CHINESE
in 10 minutes a day®

by Kristine K. Kershul, M.A., University of California, Santa Barbara

Consultants: Jiemin Wu and Howard Xie

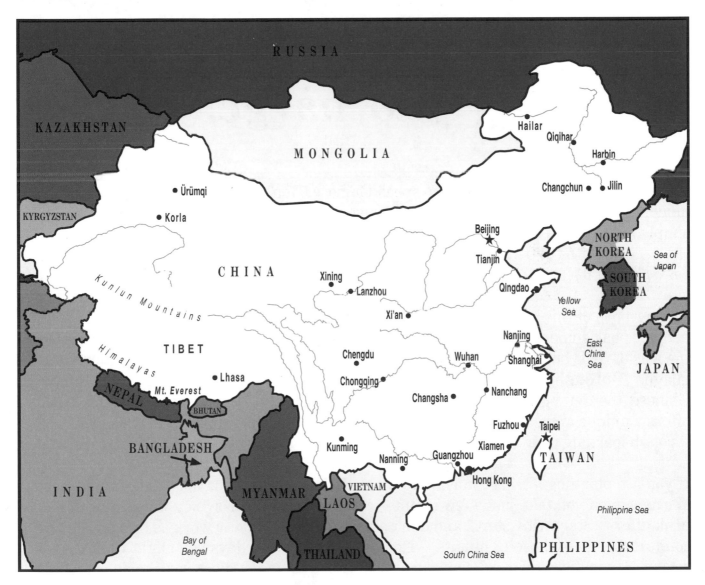

Bilingual Books, Inc.
1719 West Nickerson Street, Seattle, WA 98119
Tel: (206) 284-4211 Fax: (206) 284-3660
www.10minutesaday.com • www.bbks.com

ISBN: 978-1-931873-01-7   Third printing, January 2014

Can you say this?

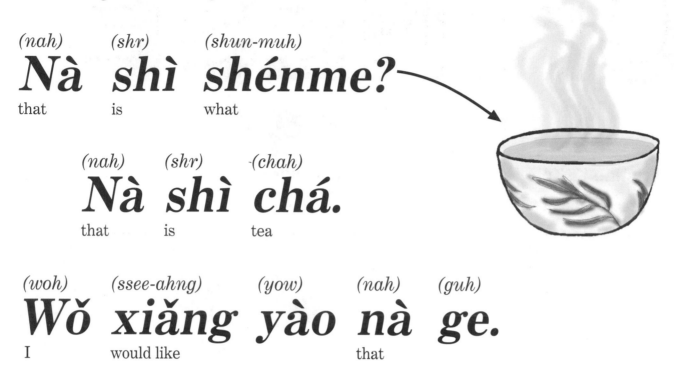

(nah)   *(shr)*   *(shun-muh)*
Nà shì shénme?
that   is   what

(nah)   *(shr)*   *-(chah)*
Nà shì chá.
that   is   tea

(woh)   *(ssee-ahng)*   *(yow)*   *(nah)*   *(guh)*
Wǒ xiǎng yào nà ge.
I   would like   that

If you can say this, you can learn to speak Chinese. You will be able to easily order beer, lunch, tea, theater tickets, or anything else you wish. With your best Chinese accent, you simply ask **"Nà shì shénme?"** *(nah) (shr) (shun-muh)* and, upon learning what it is, you can order it with **"Wǒ xiǎng yào nà ge,"** *(woh) (ssee-ahng) (yow) (nah) (guh)*. Sounds easy, doesn't it?

The purpose of this book is to give you an **immediate** speaking ability in Chinese. More people speak some form of Chinese as their native language than any other language in the world. This book is based on **Pǔtōnghuà** *(poo-tohng-hwah)* meaning "common language." **Pǔtōnghuà** is modern, standardized Chinese and derives largely from Mandarin Chinese, the Beijing dialect of Chinese. To help you master these new sounds, this book offers a unique and easy system of pronunciation above each word which walks you through learning Chinese.

If you are planning a trip or moving to where Chinese is spoken, you will be leaps ahead of everyone if you take just a few minutes a day to learn the easy key words that this book offers. Start with Step 1 and don't skip around. Each day work as far as you can comfortably go in those 10 minutes. Don't overdo it. Some days you might want to just review. If you forget a word, you can always look it up in the glossary. Spend your first 10 minutes studying the map on the previous page. And yes, have fun learning your new language.

As you work through the Steps, always use the special features which only this series offers. This book contains sticky labels and flash cards, free words, puzzles and quizzes. When you have completed this book, cut out the menu guide and take it along on your trip.

1   Pīnyīn

Pīnyīn is a system of spelling Chinese using the Roman alphabet. Throughout this book you will find an easy pronunciation guide above all new words. Practice these sounds with the examples given below which are mostly provinces or cities in China you might wish to visit. Refer to this Step whenever you need help, but remember, spend no longer than 10 minutes a day.

Chinese has four basic tones. The first time you work through this book, do not worry about them. Learn your vocabulary *first*. Once you learn the words, go back and practice with the tones.

Tone 1 is even. The voice produces a flat, somewhat higher pitch than normal. ⟶ **ā ǎ** ⟵ Tone 3 is falling and rising. The voice drops from a normal pitch to a lower pitch and then rises again.

Tone 2 is rising. The voice rises from a normal to a higher pitch. ⟶ **á à** ⟵ Tone 4 is falling. The voice falls from a high to a low pitch.

Pīnyīn letter	English sound	Examples	*Write it here*
a	ah	**Ānhuī** *(ahn-hway)*	
b	b	**Běijīng** *(bay-jeeng)*	
c	ts *(as in cats)*	**Cāngyánshān** *(tsahng-yahn-shahn)*	
ch	ch	**Chángshā** *(chahng-shah)*	*Chángshā, Chángshā*
d	d	**Hǎinán Dǎo** *(hi-nahn)(dow)* island	
e *(varies)*	uh *(as in let)*	**Érhǎi Hú** *(ur-hi)(hoo)* lake	
	eh	**Éméishān** *(eh-may-shahn)*	
f	f	**Fújiàn** *(foo-jee-ahn)*	
g	g	**Gānsù** *(yahn-soo)*	
h	h	**Húnán** *(hoo-nahn)*	
i *(varies)*	ee	**Xī'ān** *(ssee-ahn)*	
	r	**Shíwān** *(shr-wahn)*	
	uh	**Zībó** *(zuh-bwoh)*	
	ih	**Sīmǎtái Chángchéng** *(sih-mah-tie)(chahng-chuhng)* Great Wall	
j	j	**Jílín** *(jee-leen)*	
k	k	**Kūnmíng** *(koon-meeng)*	
l	l	**Lāsà** *(lah-sah)*	
m	m	**Nèi Ménggǔ** *(nay)(muhng-goo)* Inner Mongolia	
n	n	**Nánjīng** *(nahn-jeeng)*	
o *(varies)*	oh	**Tóngjiāng** *(tohng-jee-ahng)*	

3

Pīnyīn letter	English sound	Examples	Write it here
o	woh	**Fóshān** *(fwoh-shahn)*	_____
p	p	**Pánshān** *(pahn-shahn)*	_____
q	ch	**Qīngdǎo** *(cheeng-dow)*	_____
r	r	**Hāěrbīn** *(hah-ur-been)*	_____
s	s	**Sìchuān** *(sih-chwahn)*	_____
sh	sh	**Shànghǎi** *(shahng-hi)*	_____
t	t	**Tiānjīn** *(tee-ahn-jeen)*	_____
u *(varies)*	oo	**Wúhú** *(woo-hoo)*	_____
	ew	**Yúlín** *(yew-leen)*	_____
w	w	**Wǔhàn** *(woo-hahn)*	_____
x	*(a gentle hissing sound)* ss / sh	**Xiāng Gǎng** *(ssee-ahng)(gahng)* Hong Kong	_____
y	y	**Yúnnán** *(yoon-nahn)*	_____
z	z	**Zōuxiàn** *(zoh-ssee-ahn)*	_____
zh	j	**Zhèjiāng** *(juh-jee-ahng)*	_____

Many of the following sounds were used in the above examples. Here is a chance to practice these new sounds and to learn your first ten Chinese words. Don't forget to have fun learning your new language.

ai	I / eye	*(hi)* **hǎi** sea	**ua** *(varies)*	wah	*(hwah)* **huà** language
ao	*(as in how)* ow / ao	*(how)* **hǎo** good		oo-ah	*(yoo-ahn)* **yuán** unit of Chinese currency
ei	ay	*(hay)* **hēi** black	**uai**	why	*(hwhy)* **huài** bad
ou	oh	*(goh)* **gǒu** dog	**ui**	way	*(hway)* **huī** gray
ü	oo	*(noo)* **nǚ** female	**uo**	woh	*(hwoh)* **huǒ** fire

Regarding the phonetics, remember Chinese is spoken in a variety of ways. Think about how different British and American English sound. In Chinese the tones will vary or can even be absent. Sometimes words will be combined instead of being written separately. Don't let these things surprise you.

* *r* is similar to a little growl, so **shí** *(shr)* sounds almost like the English "sure"
* *oh/woh* sometimes it can be difficult to tell the difference between these sounds

The easiest and best possible phonetics have been chosen for each individual word. Pronounce the phonetics just as you see them. Don't over-analyze them.

2   Key Question Words

When you arrive in **Běijīng** *(bay-jeeng)* or **Shànghǎi** *(shahng-hi)* the very first thing you will need to do is ask

questions — "Where **nǎr** *(nahr)* is the bus stop?" "**Nǎr** *(nahr)* can I exchange money?" "**Nǎr** *(nahr)* is the

lavatory?" "**Nǎr** is a restaurant?" "**Nǎr** do I catch a taxi?" "**Nǎr** is a good hotel?" "**Nǎr** is my

luggage?" — and the list will go on and on for the entire length of your visit. In Chinese, there

are NINE KEY QUESTION WORDS to learn. For example, the nine key question words will

help you find out exactly what you are ordering in a restaurant before you order it — and not

after the surprise (or shock!) arrives. Take a few minutes to study and practice saying the nine

key question words listed below. Then cover the Chinese with your hand and fill in each of the

blanks with the matching Chinese **cí.** *(tsih)* word

(nahr) *(nah)*
NǍR / NǍ   = WHERE _____

(shun-muh)
SHÉNME   = WHAT _____

(shay) *(shway)*
SHÉI / SHÚI   = WHO *shéi, shéi, shéi, shéi*

(way-shun-muh)
WÈISHÉNME   = WHY _____

(shun-muh) *(shr-hoh)*
SHÉNME SHÍHOU   = WHEN _____

(zuhn-muh)
ZĚNME   = HOW _____

(dwoh-shao)
DUŌSHAO   = HOW MUCH _____
HOW MANY

(jee)
JǏ   = HOW MANY _____

(nay)
NĚI   = WHICH _____

5

Now test yourself to see if you really can keep these *(tsih)* **cí** (words) straight in your mind. Draw lines between the *(jwong-wuhn)* **Zhōngwén** (Chinese language) *(tsih)* **cí** (words) and their English equivalents below.

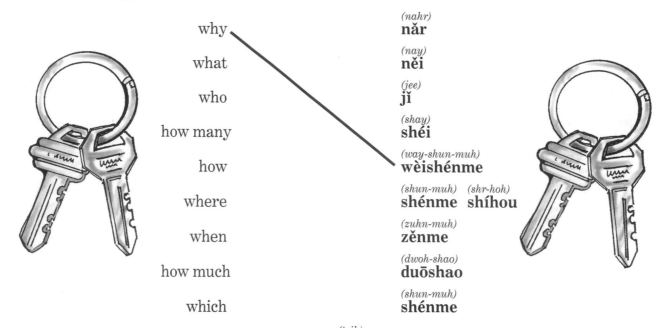

why	*(nahr)* **nǎr**
what	*(nay)* **něi**
who	*(jee)* **jǐ**
how many	*(shay)* **shéi**
how	*(way-shun-muh)* **wèishénme**
where	*(shun-muh)* **shénme** *(shr-hoh)* **shíhou**
when	*(zuhn-muh)* **zěnme**
how much	*(dwoh-shao)* **duōshao**
which	*(shun-muh)* **shénme**

Examine the following questions containing these *(tsih)* **cí**. Practice the sentences out loud and then practice by copying the Chinese in the blanks underneath each question.

(zuhn-muh) (luh)
Zěnme le?
how is wrong (what is wrong)

_____

(suh-lah) (zuhn-muh) (yahng)
Sèlā zěnme yàng?
salad   how (is it)

_____

(nah) (shr) (shay)
Nà shì shéi?
that is who

_____ *Nà shì shéi?* _____

(hwoh-chuh) (shun-muh) (shr-hoh) (lie)
Huǒchē shénme shíhou lái?
train   when   comes

_____

(juh) (guh) (dwoh-shao) (chee-ahn)
Zhè ge duōshao qián?
this (is)   how much   money

_____

(nahr) (yoh) (dee-ahn-hwah)
Nǎr yǒu diànhuà?
where is there telephone

_____

(nahr)
"Nǎr" will be your most used question *(tsih)* **cí**. Say each of the following Chinese sentences aloud. Then write out each sentence without looking at the example. If you don't succeed on the first try, don't give up. Just practice each sentence until you are able to do it easily. Remember "**ai**" is pronounced like the word "eye" or "I" and "**ao**" is pronounced "ow" as in "h<u>ow</u>."

(nahr) (yoh) (tsuh-swoh)
Nǎr yǒu cèsuǒ?
where is there lavatory

(nahr) (yoh) (choo-zoo-chuh)
Nǎr yǒu chūzūchē?
where is there taxi

(yoh) (gohng-gohng-chee-chuh)
Nǎr yǒu gōnggòngqìchē?
bus

_____ <u>Nǎr yǒu chūzūchē?</u> _____

(fahn-gwahn)
Nǎr yǒu fànguǎn?
restaurant

(yeen-hahng)
Nǎr yǒu yínháng?
bank

(loo-gwahn)
Nǎr yǒu lǚguǎn?
hotel

_____ _____ _____

Chinese and English are obviously very different languages, but some things are actually easier in Chinese. Notice how similar questions and statements are in Chinese.

(nahr) (yoh) (tsuh-swoh)
Nǎr yǒu cèsuǒ? (question)
where is there lavatory

(juhr) (yoh) (tsuh-swoh)
Zhèr yǒu cèsuǒ. (statement)
here

(shun-muh)
Shénme is a useful question **cí**. From **shénme,** come other question word combinations.
what

(shr-hoh)
shénme shíhou = what time/when _____ *shénme shíhou, shénme shíhou*

(dee-fahng)
shénme dìfāng = what place/where _____

(ruhn)
shénme rén = what person/who _____

Notice how these groups of words are built around a common element. Here it is **"zi"** pronounced *"zuh."*

☑ **chāzi** *(chah-zuh)* .... fork   *chāzi, chāzi, chāzi, chāzi, chāzi*
☐ **bēizi** *(bay-zuh)* .... cup, mug
☐ **dāozi** *(dow-zuh)* .... knife   子
☐ **kuàizi** *(kwhy-zuh)* .... chopsticks   *zi*

Additional fun **cí** like these will appear at the bottom of the following pages in a yellow color band. Say each **cí** aloud and then write out the **Zhōngwén cí** *(jwong-wuhn)* in the blank to the right.
Chinese language

(jwong-gwoh)   *(hwah)*   *(tsih)*   *(jwong-gwoh)*   *(hwah)*   *(juh)*   *(nah)*
Zhōngguó huà does not have **cí** for "the" and "a." Instead, **Zhōngguó huà** uses **zhè** and **nà**
China   language   this   that

(jwong-gwoh)   *(juh)*   *(nah)*
for "the" and nothing for "a." In **Zhōngguó huà, zhè** and **nà** reflect the item's distance from
                                              this   that

the speaker.

(juh)   *(shoo)*   *(nah)*   *(shoo)*   *(juh)*   *(jee)*   *(nah)*   *(jee)*
zhè shū vs. **nà shū**   **zhè jī** vs. **nà jī**
this   book   that   book   this   chicken   that   chicken

(juh)   *(yoo)*   *(nah)*   *(yoo)*   *(juh)*   *(dee-ahn-hwah)*   *(nah)*   *(dee-ahn-hwah)*
zhè yú vs. **nà yú**   **zhè diànhuà** vs. **nà diànhuà**
this   fish   that   this   telephone   that

(juh)   *(nah)*
In addition to **zhè** and **nà,** Chinese has "measure words" (M) or "counting words" for everything.
             this   that

(buhn)   *(tsih) (buhn)*
Běn is an example of a Chinese measure **cí. Běn,** meaning "bound together," is used with words
(M)   (M)

like "book" and "magazine."

(yee) (buhn) (shoo)   *(yee) (buhn) (zah-jihr)*
yì běn shū   **yì běn zázhì**
one (bound) book   one   (M)   magazine

Often Chinese "measure words" cannot be translated into English. Don't worry about them. You

can easily identify these "measure words" by the (M) underneath them.

In Step 2 you were introduced to the Nine Key Question Words. These nine words are the basics, the most essential building blocks for learning Chinese. Throughout this book you will come across keys asking you to fill in the missing question word. Use this opportunity not only to fill in the blank on that key, but to review all your question words. Play with the new sounds, speak slowly and have fun.

❐   **chē** *(chuh)* . . . . vehicle
❐   **chēpái** *(chuh-pie)* . . . . license plate
❐   **chēzhàn** *(chuh-jahn)* . . . . vehicle/bus stop
❐   **jípǔchē** *(jee-poo-chuh)* . . . . jeep
❐   **miànbāochē** *(mee-ahn-bao-chuh)* . . . . van

chē

Before you proceed with this Step, situate yourself comfortably in your living room. Now look around you. Can you name the things that you see in this **kètīng** *(kuh-teeng)* (living room) in Chinese? You can probably guess **shāfā** *(shah-fah)* means "sofa." Let's learn the rest of them. After practicing these **cí** *(tsih)* out loud, write them in the blanks below.

(dung)
dēng _____
lamp

(shah-fah)
shāfā _____
sofa

(yee-zuh)
yǐzi _____
chair

(dee-bahn)
dìbǎn _____
floor

(jwoh-zuh)
zhuōzi   zhuōzi, zhuōzi, zhuōzi
table

(muhn)
mén _____
door

(jwong)
zhōng _____
clock

(chah-jee)
chájī _____
coffee table

(dee-ahn-hwah)
diànhuà _____
telephone

(chwahng-hoo)
chuānghù
window

(hwahr)
huàr
picture

Remember that **Zhōngguó huà** *(hwah)* (China) has no word for "the." Use **zhè** *(juh)* or **nà** *(nah)* before the object to indicate something in particular or use a number. Even easier, don't use anything at all! Now open your **shū** *(shoo)* (book) to the sticky labels on page 17 and later on page 35. Peel off the first 11 labels and proceed around the **kètīng** *(kuh-teeng)* (living room), labeling these items in your **jiā** *(jee-ah)* (home). This will help to increase your **Zhōngwén cí** *(jwong-wahn)* *(tsih)* (Chinese language word) power easily. Don't forget to say each **cí** as you attach the label.

Now ask yourself, **"Shāfā zài nǎr?"** *(shah-fah) (zi) (nahr)* (sofa is where) and point at it while you answer, **"Shāfā zài zhèr."** *(zi) (juhr)* (is here)

Continue on down the list above until you feel comfortable with these **xīn cí.** *(sseen)* (new)

❏	**diànchē** *(dee-ahn-chuh)*	trolley	
❏	**huǒchē** *(hwoh-chuh)*	train	车 _____
❏	**qìchē** *(chee-chuh)*	car	_____
❏	**sānlúnchē** *(sahn-loon-chuh)*	pedicab	*chē* _____
❏	**zìxíngchē** *(zih-sseeng-chuh)*	bicycle	_____

9

(fahng-zuh)
fángzi = house

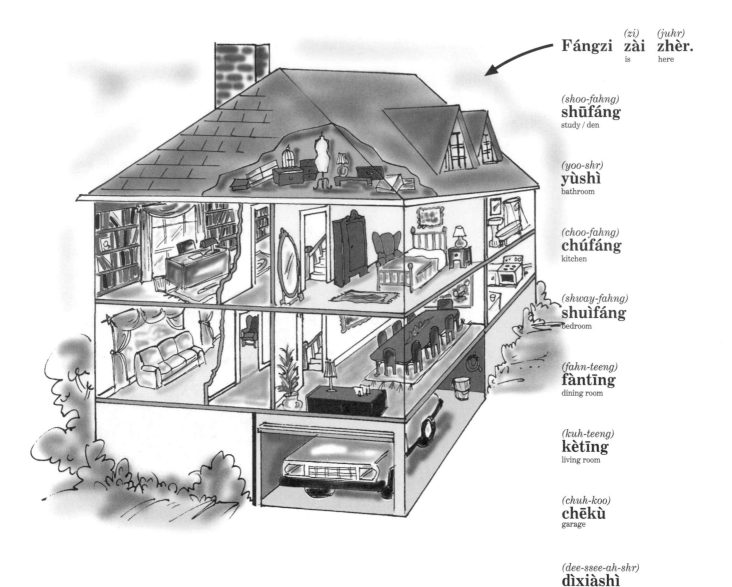

Fángzi *(zi)* **zài** *(juhr)* **zhèr.**
            is   here

(shoo-fahng)
shūfáng
study / den

(yoo-shr)
yùshì
bathroom

(choo-fahng)
chúfáng
kitchen

(shway-fahng)
shuìfáng
bedroom

(fahn-teeng)
fàntīng
dining room

(kuh-teeng)
kètīng
living room

(chuh-koo)
chēkù
garage

(dee-ssee-ah-shr)
dìxiàshì
basement

While learning these *(sseen)* **xīn** *(tsih)* **cí,** let's not forget:
                  new   words

(chee-chuh)
qìchē
car

(sahn-loon-chuh)
sānlúnchē
pedicab

(zih-sseeng-chuh)
zìxíngchē
bicycle

_____   _____   _____

☐ **bǐ** *(bee)* .... pen, writing instrument
☐ **bǐjì** *(bee-jee)* .... to take notes
☐ **bǐjī** *(bee-jee)* .... handwriting
☐ **bǐjìběn** *(bee-jee-buhn)* .... notebook
☐ **bǐxīn** *(bee-sseen)* .... pen/pencil refill

笔
bǐ

(mao)
(mao)
māo
cat

(hwah-yoo-ahn)
huāyuán
garden

(hwahr)
huār (**huàr** means picture!)
flowers

_____   huāyuán, huāyuán   _____

(goh)
gǒu
dog

(yoh-twong)
yóutǒng
mailbox

(sseen)
xìn
letters

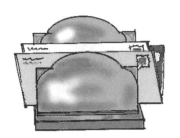

_____   _____   _____

Peel off the next set of labels and wander through your **fángzi** *(fahng-zuh)* learning these **xīn cí** *(sseen) (tsih)*. It will
                                                    house   new

be somewhat difficult to label your **gǒu,** *(goh)* **huār** *(hwahr)* or **māo** *(mao)* but be creative. Practice by asking
                                      dog   flowers   cat

yourself, "**Nǎr yǒu huāyuán?**" *(nahr) (yoh) (hwah-yoo-ahn)* and reply, "**Huāyuán zài zhèr.**" *(zi) (juhr)*
          where is there   here

Nǎr yǒu fángzi? *(yoh) (fahng-zuh)*
                    house

❑ **fěnbǐ** *(fuhn-bee)*........................	chalk	
❑ **gāngbǐ** *(gahng-bee)*....................	fountain pen	
❑ **máobǐ** *(mao-bee)*......................	writing brush	笔
❑ **qiānbǐ** *(chee-ahn-bee)*................	pencil	*bǐ*
❑ **yuánzhūbǐ** *(yoo-ahn-joo-bee)*............	ballpoint pen	

5

(yee) *(ur)* *(sahn)*
Yī, Èr, Sān!
one   two   three

Consider for a minute how important numbers are. How could you tell someone your phone number, your address or your hotel room if you had no numbers? And think of how difficult it would be if you could not understand the time, the price of a sandwich or the correct bus to take. When practicing the *(shoo-zih)* **shùzì** below, notice the similarities which have been underlined for you between *(ur)* **èr** and *(shr-ur)* **shíèr,** *(chee)* **qì** and *(shr-chee)* **shíqī,** and so on.
(numbers / two / twelve / seven / seventeen)

0	*(leeng)* **líng**	_____
1	*(yee)* **yī**	_____
2	*(ur)* *(lee-ahng)* **èr / liǎng**	_____
3	*(sahn)* **sān**	_____
4	*(sih)* **sì**	_____
5	*(woo)* **wǔ**	_____
6	*(lee-oo)* **liù**	_____
7	*(chee)* **qī**	*qī, qī, qī, qī, qī*
8	*(bah)* **bā**	_____
9	*(jee-oo)* **jiǔ**	_____
10	*(shr)* **shí**	_____

10	*(shr)* **shí**	_____
11	*(shr-yee)* **shíyī**	_____
12	*(shr-ur)* **shíèr**	_____
13	*(shr-sahn)* **shísān**	_____
14	*(shr-sih)* **shísì**	_____
15	*(shr-woo)* **shíwǔ**	_____
16	*(shr-lee-oo)* **shíliù**	_____
17	*(shr-chee)* **shíqī**	_____
18	*(shr-bah)* **shíbā**	_____
19	*(shr-jee-oo)* **shíjiǔ**	_____
20	*(ur-shr)* **èrshí**	_____

☑ **diàn** *(dee-ahn)* . . . . electricity   *diàn, diàn, diàn, diàn, diàn, diàn*
☐ **diànbào** *(dee-ahn-bao)* . . . . telegram
☐ **diànhuà** *(dee-ahn-hwah)* . . . . telephone
☐ **diànnǎo** *(dee-ahn-now)* . . . . computer   *diàn*
☐ **diàntǒng** *(dee-ahn-twong)* . . . . flashlight

Use these *(shoo-zih)* **shùzì** *numbers* on a daily basis. Count to yourself in *(jwong-gwoh)* **Zhōngguó** *(hwah)* **huà** *language* when you brush your teeth, exercise or commute to work. Fill in the blanks below according to the *(shoo-zih)* **shùzì** *numbers* given in parentheses. Now is also a good time to learn these two very important phrases. *Note:* When you count, you use "*(ur)* **èr**," *two* but when you are asked "how many" or you say "two pencils" or "two books" you use "*(lee-ahng)* **liǎng**." *two*

(woh) *(ssee-ahng)* *(yow)*
wǒ xiǎng yào _____
I   would like

(woh-muhn) *(ssee-ahng)* *(yow)*
wǒmen xiǎng yào _____
we   would like

(woh) *(ssee-ahng)* *(yow)*
Wǒ xiǎng yào _____ (10) *(jahng)* **zhāng** (M) *(meeng-sseen-pee-ahn)* **míngxìnpiàn.** postcards   *(dwoh-shao)* **Duōshao?** _____ (10)
I   would like

Wǒ xiǎng yào _____ (11) **zhāng** (M) *(yoh-pee-ow)* **yóupiào.** stamps   *(dwoh-shao)* **Duōshao?** _____ (11)

Wǒ xiǎng yào *bā* (8) *(jahng)* **zhāng** *(yoh-pee-ow)* **yóupiào.** **Duōshao?** _____ (8)
I

Wǒ xiǎng yào _____ (2) **zhāng yóupiào.** **Duōshao?** _____ (2)

(woh-muhn)
Wǒmen xiǎng yào _____ (9) **zhāng** (M) *(meeng-sseen-pee-ahn)* **míngxìnpiàn.** postcards   **Duōshao?** _____ (9)
we

Wǒmen xiǎng yào _____ (10) **zhāng míngxìnpiàn.** **Duōshao?** _____ (10)

Wǒmen xiǎng yào _____ (3) *(jahng)* **zhāng** (M) *(ssee-pee-ow)* **xìpiào.** theater tickets   **Duōshao?** _____ (3)

(woh)
Wǒ xiǎng yào _____ (4) **zhāng xìpiào.** **Duōshao?** _____ (4)
I

Wǒ xiǎng yào _____ (11) **zhāng xìpiào.** **Duōshao?** _____ (11)

Wǒmen xiǎng yào _____ (6) *(bay)* *(chah)* **bēi chá.** cup (M) tea   **Duōshao?** _____ (6)

Wǒmen xiǎng yào _____ (5) *(bay)* *(shway)* **bēi shuǐ.** (M) water   *(how many)* _____ (5)

☐ **diànchí** *(dee-ahn-chee)* .... battery
☐ **diànshì** *(dee-ahn-shr)* .... television
☐ **diàntái** *(dee-ahn-tie)* .... radio station
☐ **diàntī** *(dee-ahn-tee)* .... elevator, escalator
☐ **diànyǐng** *(dee-ahn-yeeng)* .... movie

电
diàn
_____
_____
_____
_____

13

Now see if you can translate the following thoughts into **Zhōngwén.** *(jwong-wuhn)* The answers are provided upside down at the bottom of **zhèi** *(juh-ay)* **yè.** *(yeh)*

this page

1. I would like seven postcards.

   _____

2. I would like nine stamps.

   _____

3. We would like four cups of tea.

   _____

4. We would like three theater tickets.

   _____

Review the **shùzì** *(shoo-zih)* 1 to 20. Write out your telephone number, fax number and cellular number.

Then write out a friend's telephone number and a relative's telephone number.

(2   0   6)   2   8   4   —   4   2   1   1

èr   líng   liù _____

(   ) _ _ _ _ — _ _ _ _

_____

(   ) _ _ _ _ — _ _ _ _

_____

(yahn-suh)
Yánsè
colors

(yahn-suh)
Yánsè are the same in **Zhōngguó** as they are in *(may-gwoh)* **Měiguó** — they just have different *(meeng-zuh)* **míngzì.** In
colors   America   names

Zhōngguó, there are many different customs regarding *(yahn-suh)* **yánsè.** Let's learn the basic *(yahn-suh)* **yánsè** so
                                                                                            colors   colors

when you are invited to someone's *(fahng-zuh)* **fángzi** and you want to bring flowers, you will be able to order
                                                                       house

the color you want. Once you've learned the *(yahn-suh)* **yánsè,** quiz yourself. What color are your shoes?

Your eyes? Your hair? Your house?

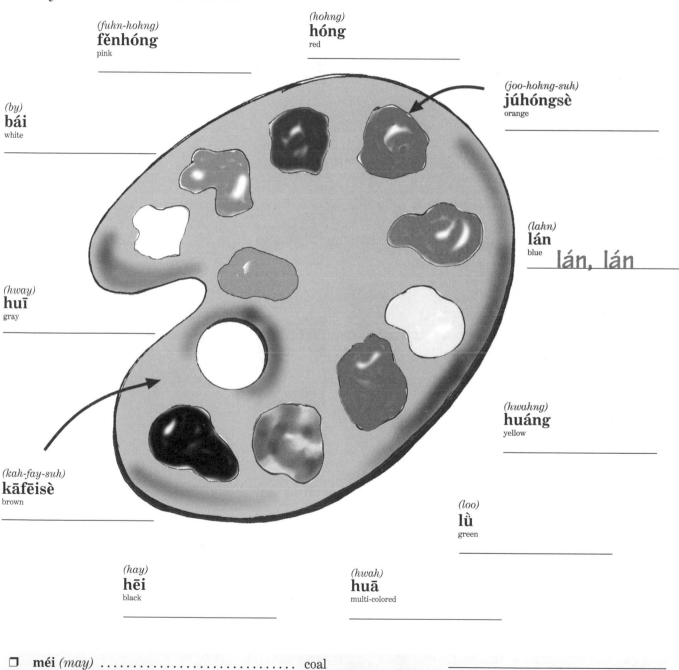

(fuhn-hohng)
fěnhóng
pink

(hohng)
hóng
red

(joo-hohng-suh)
júhóngsè
orange

(by)
bái
white

(lahn)
lán
blue   lán, lán

(hway)
huī
gray

(hwahng)
huáng
yellow

(kah-fay-suh)
kāfēisè
brown

(loo)
lù
green

(hay)
hēi
black

(hwah)
huā
multi-colored

❏ **méi** *(may)* . . . . coal
❏ **méikuàng** *(may-kwahng)* . . . . coal mine   煤
❏ **méiqì** *(may-chee)* . . . . gas
❏ **méiqìlú** *(may-chee-loo)* . . . . gas stove   *méi*
❏ **méiyóu** *(may-yoh)* . . . . kerosene

Peel off the next group of labels and proceed to label these **yánsè** in your **fángzi.** *(fahng-zuh)* Identify the
house
two or three dominant colors in the flags below.

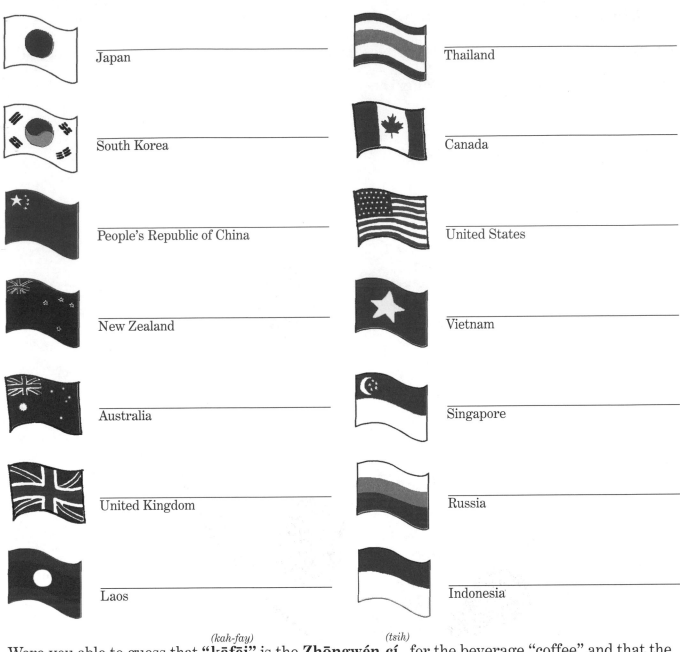

_____ Japan

_____ Thailand

_____ South Korea

_____ Canada

_____ People's Republic of China

_____ United States

_____ New Zealand

_____ Vietnam

_____ Australia

_____ Singapore

_____ United Kingdom

_____ Russia

_____ Laos

_____ Indonesia

Were you able to guess that **"kāfēi"** *(kah-fay)* is the **Zhōngwén cí** *(tsih)* for the beverage "coffee" and that the
word
cí "kāfēisè" *(kah-fay-suh)* actually means "coffee-colored?"
brown

_____ **yǒu chūzūchē?** *(yoh) (choo-zoo-chuh)*
(where)   (where)   taxi

Nà shì *(shr)* _____ ?
(what)   that   (what)

☐ **xǐ** *(ssee)* .... to wash
☐ **xǐjiāojuǎn** *(ssee-jee-ow-joo-ahn)* .... to develop (the) film
☐ **xǐyī diàn** *(ssee-yee)(dee-ahn)* .... laundry
☐ **xǐyīfú** *(ssee-yee-foo)* .... to do laundry
☐ **xǐzǎo** *(ssee-zow)* .... to take a bath

_____
_____
洗
xǐ

16

(dung) **dēng**	*(chee-chuh)* **qìchē**	*(fuhn-hohng)* **fěnhóng**	*(pee-jee-ow)* **píjiǔ**
(shah-fah) **shāfā**	*(sahn-loon-chuh)* **sānlúnchē**	*(hohng)* **hóng**	*(nee-oo-ni)* **niúnǎi**
(yee-zuh) **yǐzi**	*(zih-sseeng-chuh)* **zìxíngchē**	*(by)* **bái**	*(nee-oo-yoh)* **niúyóu**
(dee-bahn) **dìbǎn**	*(mao)* **māo**	*(joo-hohng-suh)* **júhóngsè**	*(yahn)* **yán**
(jwoh-zuh) **zhuōzi**	*(hwah-yoo-ahn)* **huāyuán**	*(lahn)* **lán**	*(hoo-jee-ow)* **hújiāo**
(muhn) **mén**	*(hwahr)* **huār**	*(hway)* **huī**	*(jee-oo-bay)* **jiǔbēi**
(jwong) **zhōng**	*(goh)* **gǒu**	*(hwahng)* **huáng**	*(bwoh-lee-bay)* **bōlíbēi**
(chah-jee) **chájī**	*(yoh-twong)* **yóutǒng**	*(kah-fay-suh)* **kāfēisè**	*(kwhy-zuh)* **kuàizi**
(dee-ahn-hwah) **diànhuà**	*(sseen)* **xìn**	*(hay)* **hēi**	*(bao-jihr)* **bàozhǐ**
(chwahng-hoo) **chuānghù**	0 *(leeng)* **líng**	*(hwah)* **huā**	*(chah-bay)* **chábēi**
(hwahr) **huàr**	1 *(yee)* **yī**	*(loo)* **lǜ**	*(tsahn-jeen)* **cānjīn**
(fahng-zuh) **fángzi**	2 *(ur)* **èr**	*(neen) (zow)* **nín zǎo**	*(chah-zuh)* **chāzi**
(shoo-fahng) **shūfáng**	3 *(sahn)* **sān**	*(wahn-shahng) (jee-ahn)* **wǎnshàng jiàn**	*(pahn-zuh)* **pánzi**
(yoo-shr) **yùshì**	4 *(sih)* **sì**	*(meeng-tee-ahn) (jee-ahn)* **míngtiān jiàn**	*(dow-zuh)* **dāozi**
(choo-fahng) **chúfáng**	5 *(woo)* **wǔ**	*(wahn) (ahn)* **wǎn ān**	*(tahng-chr)* **tāngchí**
(shway-fahng) **shuìfáng**	6 *(lee-oo)* **liù**	*(zi-jee-ahn)* **zàijiàn**	*(gway-zuh)* **guìzi**
(fahn-teeng) **fàntīng**	7 *(chee)* **qī**	*(nee) (how) (mah)* **Nǐ hǎo ma?**	*(chah)* **chá**
(kuh-teeng) **kètīng**	8 *(bah)* **bā**	*(beeng-ssee-ahng)* **bīngxiāng**	*(kah-fay)* **kāfēi**
(chuh-koo) **chēkù**	9 *(jee-oo)* **jiǔ**	*(loo-zuh)* **lúzi**	*(mee-ahn-bao)* **miànbāo**
(dee-ssee-ah-shr) **dìxiàshì**	10 *(shr)* **shí**	*(jee-oo)* **jiǔ**	*(cheeng)* **qǐng**

STICKY LABELS

This book has over 150 special sticky labels for you to use as you learn new words. When you are introduced to one of these words, remove the corresponding label from these pages. Be sure to use each of these unique self-adhesive labels by adhering them to a picture, window, lamp, or whatever object they refer to. And yes, they are removable! The sticky labels make learning to speak Chinese much more fun and a lot easier than you ever expected. For example, when you look in the mirror and see the label, say

(jeeng-zuh)
"jìngzi."
mirror

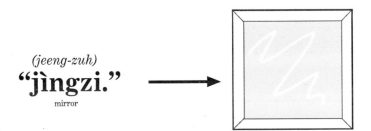

Don't just say it once, say it again and again. And once you label the refrigerator, you should never again open that door without saying

(beeng-see-ahng)
"bīngxiāng."
refrigerator

By using the sticky labels, you not only learn new words, but friends and family learn along with you! The sooner you start, the sooner you can use these labels at home or work.

7   (chee-ahn) **Qián**
money

Before starting this Step, go back and review Step 5. It is important that you can count to (ur-shr) **èrshí** twenty

without looking at the (shoo) **shū**. book Let's learn the larger (shoo-zih) **shùzì** numbers now. After practicing aloud the

(jwong-wuhn) **Zhōngwén** Chinese (shoo-zih) **shùzì** 10 through 1,000 below, write these **shùzì** (shoo-zih) in the blanks provided. Again, notice

the similarities (underlined) between numbers such as <u>wǔ</u> (woo) (5), shí<u>wǔ</u> (shr-woo) (15), and <u>wǔ</u>shí (woo-shr) (50). Don't

be surprised when you hear **liǎng** (lee-ahng) used for the number two, for example, **liǎngbǎi** (lee-ahng-by) two hundred or **èrbǎi.** (ur-by) two hundred

First learn the numbers below, then you can practice all the numbers in between them!

(shr) 10 shí	_____	(yee-by) 100 yìbǎi	_____
(ur-shr) 20 èrshí	_____	200 èrbǎi	_____
(sahn-shr) 30 sānshí	_____	300 sānbǎi	*sānbǎi, sānbǎi*
(sih-shr) 40 sìshí	_____	400 sìbǎi	_____
(woo-shr) 50 wǔshí	_____	(woo-by) 500 wǔbǎi	_____
(lee-oo-shr) 60 liùshí	_____	600 liùbǎi	_____
(chee-shr) 70 qīshí	_____	700 qībǎi	_____
(bah-shr) 80 bāshí	_____	800 bābǎi	_____
(jee-oo-shr) 90 jiǔshí	_____	(jee-oo-by) 900 jiǔbǎi	_____
(yee-by) 100 yìbǎi	_____	(yee-chee-ahn) 1000 yìqiān	_____

Here are **liǎng** (lee-ahng) two important phrases to go with all these **shùzì.** (shoo-zih) Say them out loud over and over

and then write them out twice as many times.

(woh) (yoh)
wǒ yǒu _____
I   have

(woh-muhn)
wǒmen yǒu _____
we   have

Note: In **Zhōngguó huà, "yǒu"** (yoh) means both "to have" and "there is/there are." It may seem a

bit odd at first, but you'll get the hang of it. Don't worry.

❐ **nián** *(nee-ahn)* . . . . year
❐ **jīn nián** *(jeen)(nee-ahn)* . . . . this year
❐ **míng nián** *(meeng)(nee-ahn)* . . . . next year
❐ **qù nián** *(choo)(nee-ahn)* . . . . last year
❐ **sān nián** *(sahn)(nee-ahn)* . . . . three years

年
nián

_____
_____
_____

The unit of currency in **Zhōngguó** *(jwong-gwoh)* _{China} is the **yuán.** *(yoo-ahn)* Just as in **Měiguó** *(may-gwoh)* _{America} where a dollar can be broken down into 100 pennies, the **yuán** *(yoo-ahn)* can be broken down into 100 **fēn.** *(fuhn)* The **yuán** *(yoo-ahn)* can also be broken down into 10 **jiǎo** *(jee-ow)* or **máo.** *(mao)* **Jiǎo, máo** *(jee-ow) (mao)* and **fēn** *(fuhn)* are also called **língqián.** *(leeng-chee-ahn)* _{change} Currency regulations do change frequently. Check with your local foreign-exchange office about exchanging your currency for **yuán.** *(yoo-ahn)* Study the pictures below to familiarize yourself with the various bills and coins. **Fēn** do exist, but are used infrequently. Confused? Think of a **jiǎo** *(jee-ow)* as a dime, as there are ten **jiǎo** *(jee-ow)* to a **yuán** just as there are ten dimes to an American dollar.

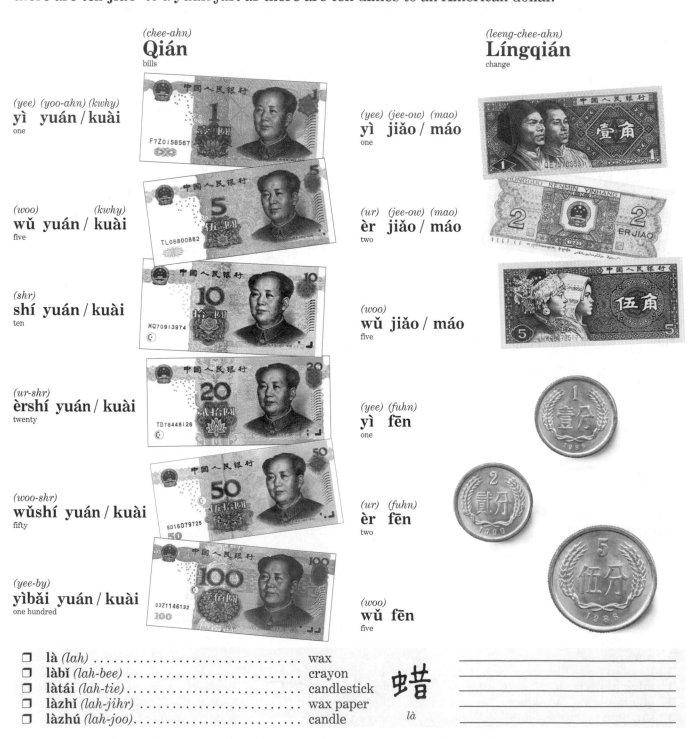

(chee-ahn)
Qián
bills

(yee) (yoo-ahn) (kwhy)
yì yuán / kuài
one

(woo) (kwhy)
wǔ yuán / kuài
five

(shr)
shí yuán / kuài
ten

(ur-shr)
èrshí yuán / kuài
twenty

(woo-shr)
wǔshí yuán / kuài
fifty

(yee-by)
yìbǎi yuán / kuài
one hundred

(leeng-chee-ahn)
Língqián
change

(yee) (jee-ow) (mao)
yì jiǎo / máo
one

(ur) (jee-ow) (mao)
èr jiǎo / máo
two

(woo)
wǔ jiǎo / máo
five

(yee) (fuhn)
yì fēn
one

(ur) (fuhn)
èr fēn
two

(woo)
wǔ fēn
five

❑ **là** *(lah)*	. . . .	wax	
❑ **làbǐ** *(lah-bee)*	. . . .	crayon	蜡
❑ **làtái** *(lah-tie)*	. . . .	candlestick	
❑ **làzhǐ** *(lah-jihr)*	. . . .	wax paper	*là*
❑ **làzhú** *(lah-joo)*	. . . .	candle	

Review the **shùzì** *(shoo-zih)* **shí** *(shr)* through **yìqiān** *(yee-chee-ahn)* again. Now, in **Zhōngwén,** *(jwong-wuhn)* how do you say "twenty-two"
numbers   ten   one thousand

or "fifty-three"? You actually do a bit of arithmetic – 5 times 10 plus 3 equals 53.   *(wǔ   x   shí)   +   sān   =   wǔshísān)*   See if you

can say and write out the **shùzì** *(shoo-zih)* on **zhèi** *(juh-ay)* **yè.** *(yeh)* The answers **zài** *(zi)* the bottom of the **yè.** *(yeh)*
this   are (at)   page

1. _____
   (25 = 2 x 10 + 5)

2. _____
   (83 = 8 x 10 + 3)

3. _____
   (47 = 4 x 10 + 7)

4. _____
   (96 = 9 x 10 + 6)

Now, how would you say the following in **Zhōngguó** *(jwong-gwoh)* **huà?** *(hwah)*
                                         Chinese   language

5. _____
   (I have 80 yuán.)

6. _____
   (We have 72 yuán.)

To ask how much something costs in **Zhōngguó huà,** one asks — **Duōshao** *(dwoh-shao)* **qián?** *(chee-ahn)*
                                                                  how much   money

Xiànzài *(ssee-ahn-zi)* you try it. _____
now   (How much money/How much does that cost?)

Answer the following questions based on the numbers in parentheses.

7. **Nà** *(nah)* **ge** *(guh)* **duōshao** *(dwoh-shao)* **qián?** *(chee-ahn)* **Nà** *(nah)* **ge** *(guh)* _____ **yuán.** *(yoo-ahn)*
   that   how much   money   that   (10)

8. **Nà běn** *(buhn)* **shū** *(shoo)* **duōshao qián? Nà běn shū** _____ **yuán.**
   (M)   book   (17)

9. **Nà zhāng** *(jahng)* **míngxìnpiàn** *(meeng-sseen-pee-ahn)* **duōshao qián? Nà zhāng míngxìnpiàn** ___ **yuán.**
   (M)   postcard   (M)   (20)

10. **Nà zhāng** *(jahng)* **zhàopiàn** *(jow-pee-ahn)* **duōshao qián? Nà zhāng zhàopiàn** _____ **yuán.**
    (M)   photo   (M)   photo   (34)

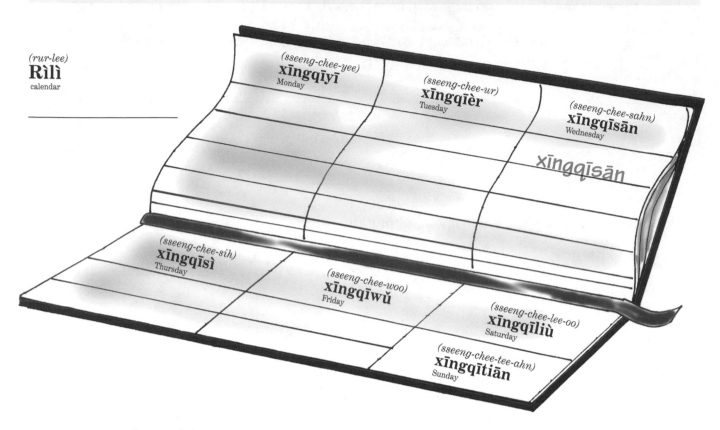

(rur-lee)
Rìlì
calendar

_____

(sseeng-chee-yee)
xīngqīyī
Monday

(sseeng-chee-ur)
xīngqīèr
Tuesday

(sseeng-chee-sahn)
xīngqīsān
Wednesday

xīngqīsān

(sseeng-chee-sih)
xīngqīsì
Thursday

(sseeng-chee-woo)
xīngqīwǔ
Friday

(sseeng-chee-lee-oo)
xīngqīliù
Saturday

(sseeng-chee-tee-ahn)
xīngqītiān
Sunday

(jwong-wuhn) *(sseeng-chee)*
Notice that in **Zhōngwén,** the days of the week are indicated by **"xīngqī"** plus a number. Learn
week

(sseeng-chee) *(rur-lee)* *(sih) (guh)*
the days of the **xīngqī** by writing them in the **rìlì** above and then move on to the **sì ge** parts
four (M)

(tee-ahn)
to each **tiān.**
day

(shahng-woo)
shàngwǔ
morning

(ssee-ah-woo)
xiàwǔ
afternoon

(wahn-shahng)
wǎnshàng
evening

(yeh-lee)
yèlǐ
night

_____   _____

❑ **cài** *(tsi)* . . . . vegetable
❑ **báicài** *(by-tsi)* . . . . cabbage
❑ **bōcài** *(bwoh-tsi)* . . . . spinach   菜
❑ **qíncài** *(cheen-tsi)* . . . . celery
❑ **shēngcài** *(shuhng-tsi)* . . . . lettuce   *cài*

It is very important to know the days of the **xīngqī** *(sseeng-chee)* week and the various parts of the **tiān** *(tee-ahn)* day as well as these **sān cí**.

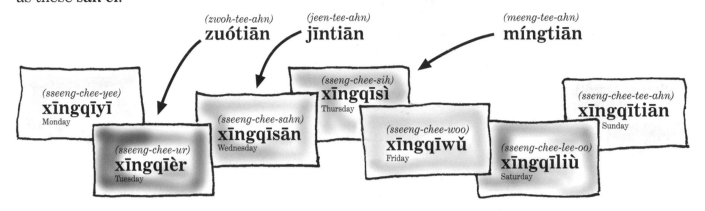

(zwoh-tee-ahn) **zuótiān**   *(jeen-tee-ahn)* **jīntiān**   *(meeng-tee-ahn)* **míngtiān**

(sseeng-chee-yee) **xīngqīyī** Monday

(sseeng-chee-ur) **xīngqīèr** Tuesday

(sseeng-chee-sahn) **xīngqīsān** Wednesday

(sseng-chee-sih) **xīngqīsì** Thursday

(sseeng-chee-woo) **xīngqīwǔ** Friday

(sseeng-chee-lee-oo) **xīngqīliù** Saturday

(sseeng-chee-tee-ahn) **xīngqītiān** Sunday

(jeen-tee-ahn) (shr) **Jīntiān shì** _____ .
(?)

(meeng-tee-ahn) **Míngtiān shì** _____ .
(?)

(zwoh-tee-ahn) **Zuótiān shì** _____ .
yesterday (?)

Xiànzài, fill in the following blanks and then check your answers at the bottom of **zhèi** *(juh-ay)* this **yè.** *(yeh)* Starting from **xiànzài,** *(ssee-ahn-zi)* now Monday **shì** *(shr)* "**xīngqīyī.**" *(sseeng-chee-yee)*

a.   Sunday morning   =   _____

b.   Friday morning   =   _____

c.   Saturday evening   =   _____

d.   Thursday afternoon   =   _____ *xīngqīsì xiàwǔ* _____

e.   Thursday night   =   _____

f.   yesterday evening   =   _____

g.   tomorrow afternoon   =   _____

h.   tomorrow evening   =   _____

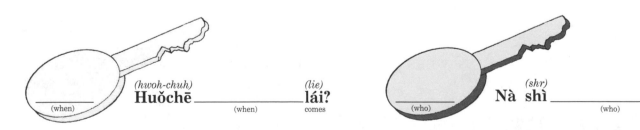

_____ **Huǒchē** *(hwoh-chuh)* _____ **lái?** *(lie)* comes
(when)   (when)

_____ **Nà shì** *(shr)* _____ ?
(who)   (who)

ANSWERS

a. xīngqītiān shàngwǔ	d. xīngqīsì xiàwǔ	g. míngtiān xiàwǔ
b. xīngqīwǔ shàngwǔ	e. xīngqīsì yèlǐ	h. míngtiān wǎnshàng
c. xīngqīliù wǎnshàng	f. zuótiān wǎnshàng	

23

Knowing the parts of the **tiān** *(tee-ahn)* / day will help you to learn the various greetings in **Zhōngguó huà.** *(jwong-gwoh)* / Chinese language

Practice these every day until your trip.

(neen) (zow)
nín zǎo _____
good morning

(wahn-shahng) (jee-ahn)
wǎnshàng jiàn _____
see you in the evening

(jee-ahn)
míngtiān jiàn _____
see you tomorrow

(wahn) (ahn)
wǎn ān _____
good night

(zi-jee-ahn)
zàijiàn _____
good-bye / see you later

Take the next group of labels and stick them on the appropriate **dōngxi** *(dwong-ssee)* / things in your **fángzi.** *(fahng-zuh)* / house Make sure you attach them to the correct items, as they are only in **Zhōngguó huà.** *(hwah)* How about the bathroom mirror for **wǎnshàng jiàn?** *(wahn-shahng)* Or your alarm clock for **míngtiān jiàn?** Let's not forget,

(nee) (how) (mah)
Nǐ hǎo ma? _____
how are you

Now for some "**shì**" *(shr)* / yes or " **bù**" *(boo)* / no questions –

Are your eyes **lán?** *(lahn)* _____ Are your shoes **kāfēisè?** *(kah-fay-suh)* _____

Is your favorite color **hóng?** *(hohng)* _____ Is today **xīngqīliù?** *(sseeng-chee-lee-oo)* _____

Do you own a **gǒu?** *(goh)* _____ Do you own a **māo?** *(mao)* _____

You are about one-fourth of your way through **zhèi** *(juh-ay)* / this **běn** *(buhn)* / (M) **shū** *(shoo)* / book and it is a good time to quickly review the **cí** you have learned before doing the crossword puzzle on the next **yè.** *(yeh)* When you do the crossword puzzles in this book, do not worry about the tones, focus on the words first and foremost.

ANSWERS TO THE CROSSWORD PUZZLE

ACROSS

16. shì
15. kāfēisè
14. chá
10. huāyuán
8. xiǎo
6. xiàwu
5. míngzi
4. dēng

17. huì
19. wǒmen
21. gōnggòngqìchē
25. huàr
27. diànhuà
28. fángzi
29. lǜguǎn
33. nián

35. shuǐ
36. huáng
37. èr

DOWN

1. zìxíngchē
2. qìchē
3. cài
4. duōshao
5. māo
7. gǒu
8. xìn
9. yánsè

11. yínháng
12. liǎng
13. cèsuǒ
15. kètīng
17. hóng
18. jīntiān
20. hēi
22. chuānghu

23. shūzi
24. xīngqī
26. rìlì
30. gāngbǐ
31. yǐzi
32. shù
34. nàr

24

CROSSWORD PUZZLE

The crossword grid contains the filled answer at 5 Across: **m í n g z ì**

ACROSS

4. lamp, light	**17.** gray	**33.** year
5. name	**19.** we	**35.** water
6. afternoon	**21.** bus	**36.** yellow
8. theater ticket	**25.** flower	**37.** two, second
10. garden	**27.** telephone,	
14. tea	telephone call	
15. brown	**28.** house	
16. ten	**29.** hotel	

DOWN

1. bicycle	**9.** color	**22.** window
2. car	**11.** bank	**23.** number
3. vegetables	**12.** two	**24.** week
4. how much,	**13.** lavatory	**26.** calendar
how many	**15.** living room	**30.** fountain pen
5. cat	**17.** red	**31.** chair
7. dog	**18.** today	**32.** book
8. new	**20.** black	**34.** where

❏ **càidān** *(tsi-dahn)* . . . . menu
❏ **càihuā** *(tsi-hwah)* . . . . cauliflower
❏ **càiyuán** *(tsi-yoo-ahn)* . . . . vegetable garden
❏ **càiyóu** *(tsi-yoh)* . . . . vegetable oil
❏ **càizǐr** *(tsi-zur)* . . . . vegetable seeds

菜

cài

9

(lee)   *(shahng)*   *(tswong)*
Lǐ,   Shàng,   Cóng . . .
inside   on   from

(jwong-gwoh)
Prepositions in **Zhōngguó huà** (words like "in," "on," "through" and "next to") are easy to
language

learn, and they allow you to be precise with a minimum of effort. Instead of having to point **liù**

times at a yummy snack you would like to purchase, you can explain precisely which one you

(zi)
want by saying **zài** behind, in front of or under whatever the salesperson is starting to pick
it is

up. Let's learn some of these little **cí**.

(ssee-ah-bee-ahn)
xiàbiān _____
under side (under)

(jeen)
jìn _____
into / in

(shahng-bee-ahn)
shàngbiān _____
top   side (over)

(lee)
lǐ _____
inside

(chee-ahn-bee-ahn)
qiánbiān ___ qiánbiān, qiánbiān ___
front   side (in front of)

(hoh-bee-ahn)
hòubiān _____
rear   side (behind)

(pahng-bee-ahn)
pángbiān _____
by   side (next to)

(tswong)
cóng _____
out of / from

(shahng)
shàng _____
on / on top of

(dee-ahn-sseen)
diǎnxīn _____
snack!

(bee-ahn)
Did you notice that many of these words contain the word **"biān"** meaning "side"? Fill in the

(yeh)
blanks on the next **yè** with the correct prepositions.

___(how)___   *(juh)* *(guh)*   *(yahng)*
Zhè ge ____(how)____ **yàng?**
this (is)

___(why)___   ____(why)____   *(hwoh-chuh) (boo) (lie)*
huǒchē bù lái?
train   not   come

- ❑ **shíwù** *(shr-woo)* . . . . food _____
- ❑ **shípǔ** *(shr-poo)* . . . . cookbook, recipes
- ❑ **shíyù** *(shr-yoo)* . . . . appetite
- ❑ **shízhǐ** *(shr-jihr)* . . . . index finger
- ❑ **shísù** *(shr-soo)* . . . . room and board

食
shí
_____
_____
_____

Nà *(dee-ahn-sseen)* **diǎnxīn** *(zi)* **zài** *(jwoh-zuh)* **zhuōzi** _____ .
that   pastry   is   table   (on)

Nà ge *(yee-shuhng)* **yīshēng** *(zi)* **zài nà ge** *(loo-gwahn)* **lǚguǎn** _____ .
(M) doctor   is   hotel   (inside)

Nà ge *(nahn-ruhn)* **nánrén zài nà ge** *(loo-gwahn)* **lǚguǎn** _____ .
that (M) man   hotel   (in front of)

Nà ge *(dee-ahn-hwah)* **diànhuà** *(hwahr)* **zài huàr** _____ .
telephone   picture   (next to)

Nà ge *(goh)* **gǒu zài** *(jwoh-zuh)* **zhuōzi** _____ .
dog   table   (under)

Nà ge *(yee-shuhng)* **yīshēng zài nǎr?** _____
that (M)

Nà ge nánrén zài nǎr? _____

Nà ge diànhuà zài nǎr? _____

(ssee-ahn-zi)
Xiànzài, fill in each blank on the picture below with the best possible one of these little **cí.**
now

Hopefully you will enjoy many Chinese gardens similar to the one below.

❏	**guó** *(gwoh)*	nation, state	
❏	**Fǎguó** *(fah-gwoh)*	France	
❏	**Měiguó** *(may-gwoh)*	United States	
❏	**Yīngguó** *(yeeng-gwoh)*	England	
❏	**Zhōngguó** *(jwong-gwoh)*	China	

国. guó

You have learned the days of the *(sseeng-chee)* **xīngqī,** so *(ssee-ahn-zi)* **xiànzài** it is time to learn the *(yoo-eh)* **yuè** of the *(nee-ahn)* **nián** and
week   now   months   year

all the different kinds of *(tee-ahn-chee)* **tiānqì.**
weather

(yee-yoo-eh) **yīyuè**	*(ur-yoo-eh)* **èryuè**	*(sahn-yoo-eh)* **sānyuè**	*(sih-yoo-eh)* **sìyuè**
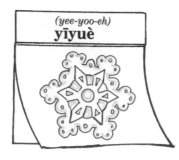		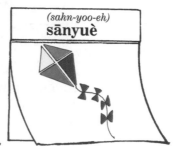	
(woo-yoo-eh) **wǔyuè**	*(lee-oo-yoo-eh)* **liùyuè**	*(chee-yoo-eh)* **qīyuè**	*(bah-yoo-eh)* **bāyuè**

(jee-oo-yoo-eh) **jiǔyuè**	*(shr-yoo-eh)* **shíyuè**	*(shr-yee-yoo-eh)* **shíyīyuè**	*(shr-ur-yoo-eh)* **shíèryuè**

When you ask about the *(tee-ahn-chee)* **tiānqì** in **Zhōngwén,** you ask a little differently than you do in
weather

(yeeng-wuhn)   *(jeen-tee-ahn)* *(tee-ahn-chee)* *(zuhn-muh)* *(yahng)*
Yīngwén – "Jīntiān tiānqì zěnme yàng?" – and you have a variety of answers. Let's
English   today   weather   how

learn them but first, does this sound familiar?

(sih-yoo-eh) **Sìyuè,**	*(lee-oo-yoo-eh)* **liùyuè,**	*(jee-oo-yoo-eh)* **jiǔyuè,**	*(shr-yee-yoo-eh)* **shíyīyuè,**	*(doh)* **dōu**	*(yoh)* **yǒu**	*(sahn-shr)* **sānshí**	**tiān.**
April	June	September	November	all	have	30	days

☐ **guógē** *(gwoh-guh)* . . . . national anthem
☐ **guóhuì** *(gwoh-hway)* . . . . parliament
☐ **guójí** *(gwoh-jee)* . . . . nationality
☐ **guójiā** *(gwoh-jee-ah)* . . . . country
☐ **guómín** *(gwoh-meen)* . . . . people of a country

guó

_____
_____
_____
_____
_____

(jeen-tee-ahn) (tee-ahn-chee) (zuhn-muh) (yahng)
Jīntiān tiānqì zěnme yàng? _____
today   weather   how   kind

(yee-yoo-eh) (ssee-ah-ssee-yoo-eh)
Yīyuè xiàxuě. _____
         (it) snows

(ur-yoo-eh) (yuh) (ssee-ah-ssee-yoo-eh)
Èryuè yě xiàxuě. _____
       also

(ssee-ah-yoo)
Sānyuè xiàyǔ. _____
         rains

(sih-yoo-eh) (ssee-ah-yoo)
Sìyuè yě xiàyǔ. _____
        also rains

(gwah-fung)
Wǔyuè guāfēng. _____
         windy

(lee-oo-yoo-eh) (yuh) (gwah-fung)
Liùyuè yě guāfēng. _____

(chee-yoo-eh) (huhn) (noo-ahn-hwoh)
Qīyuè hěn nuǎnhuo. _____
         very   warm

(bah-yoo-eh) (huhn) (ruh)
Bāyuè hěn rè. _____
        very hot

(jee-oo-yoo-eh) (tee-ahn-chee) (how)
Jiǔyuè tiānqì hǎo. _____
         weather good

(shr-yoo-eh) (tee-ahn-chee) (chahng-chahng) (how)
Shíyuè tiānqì chángcháng hǎo. _____
                         usually

(shr-yee-yoo-eh) (huhn) (lung)
Shíyīyuè hěn lěng. _____
            very cold

(shr-ur-yoo-eh) (tee-ahn-chee) (boo)(how)
Shíèryuè tiānqì hěn bù hǎo. _____
            weather   very not good

(ur-yoo-eh) (yahng)
Èryuè tiānqì zěnme yàng? _____
       weather   how   kind

(sih-yoo-eh)
Sìyuè tiānqì zěnme yàng? *Sìyuè xiàyǔ. Sìyuè xiàyǔ. Sìyuè xiàyǔ.*
April   how   kind

(woo-yoo-eh)
Wǔyuè tiānqì zěnme yàng? _____

(bah-yoo-eh)
Bāyuè tiānqì zěnme yàng? _____

- ❏ **guónèi** *(gwoh-nay)* . . . . domestic
- ❏ **guóqí** *(gwoh-chee)* . . . . national flag
- ❏ **guówài** *(gwoh-why)* . . . . overseas
- ❏ **guówáng** *(gwoh-wahng)* . . . . king
- ❏ **guóyíng** *(gwoh-yeeng)* . . . . state-owned

王

guó

_____
_____
_____
_____
_____

Xiànzài for the seasons of the **nián**...
(nee-ahn)
year

(dwong-tee-ahn)
dōngtiān
winter

(ssee-ah-tee-ahn)
xiàtiān
summer

(chee-yoo-tee-ahn)
qiūtiān
autumn

(choon-tee-ahn)
chūntiān
spring

(shuh-shr)
shèshì
Centigrade

(hwah-shr)
huáshì
Fahrenheit

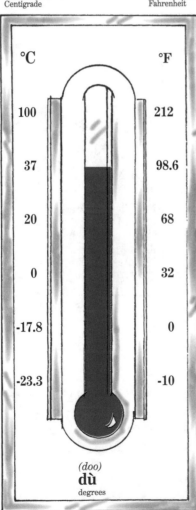

°C	°F
100	212
37	98.6
20	68
0	32
-17.8	0
-23.3	-10

(doo)
dù
degrees

At this point, it is a good time to familiarize yourself with **Zhōngguó qìwēn**. *(chee-wuhn)* temperatures Carefully study the thermometer because temperatures in **Zhōngguó** are calculated on the basis of Centigrade (not Fahrenheit).

To convert °F to °C, subtract 32 and multiply by 0.55.

98.6 °F - 32 = 66.6 x 0.55 = 37 °C

To convert °C to °F, multiply by 1.8 and add 32.

37 °C x 1.8 = 66.6 + 32 = 98.6 °F

(shuh-shr)
What is normal body temperature in **shèshì?**

What is the freezing point in **shèshì?**

☐ **wén** *(wuhn)*	written language	
☐ **Déwén** *(duh-wuhn)*	German	
☐ **Fǎwén** *(fah-wuhn)*	French	
☐ **Yīngwén** *(yeeng-wuhn)*	English	
☐ **Zhōngwén** *(jwong-wuhn)*	Chinese	

wén

(jee-ah) *(jee-ah-teeng)*

Jiā – Jiātíng
home   family

Study the family tree below. Notice that, in **Zhōngguó,** the family name comes first, and the given name (or what we, in **Měiguó,** *(may-gwoh)* think of as the first name) follows. Also, women keep their given or maiden name when they marry.
America

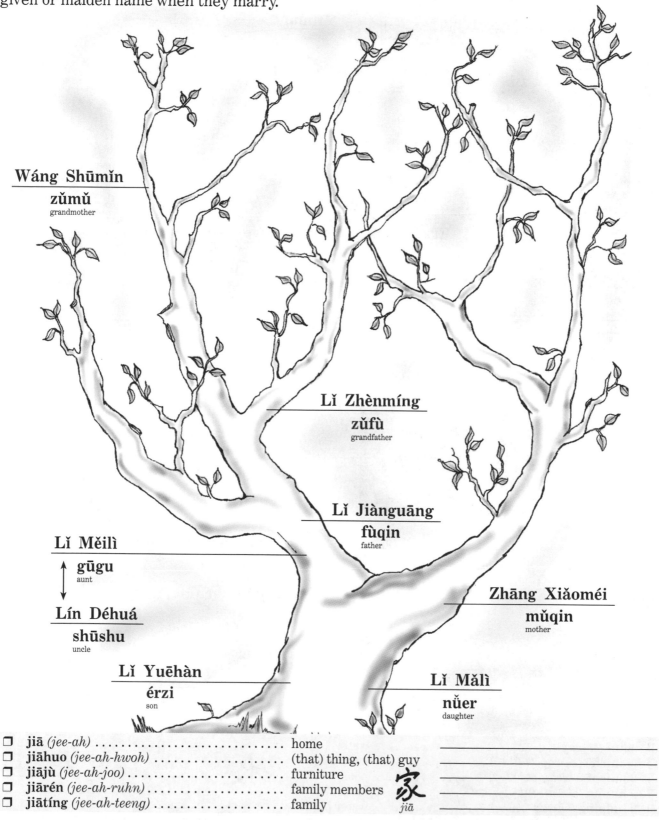

Wáng Shūmǐn

zǔmǔ
grandmother

Lǐ Zhènmíng

zǔfù
grandfather

Lǐ Jiànguāng

fùqin
father

Lǐ Měilì

gūgu
aunt

Lín Déhuá

shūshu
uncle

Zhāng Xiǎoméi

mǔqin
mother

Lǐ Yuēhàn

érzi
son

Lǐ Mǎlì

nǚer
daughter

❏ **jiā** *(jee-ah)* . . . . home _____
❏ **jiāhuo** *(jee-ah-hwoh)* . . . . (that) thing, (that) guy _____
❏ **jiājù** *(jee-ah-joo)* . . . . furniture _____
❏ **jiārén** *(jee-ah-ruhn)* . . . . family members 家 _____
❏ **jiātíng** *(jee-ah-teeng)* . . . . family *jiā* _____

Let's learn **zěnme** to identify family members by *(meeng-zuh)* **míngzì**. Study the following examples carefully.
how *name*

(nee) (jee-ow)   *(meeng-zuh)*
Nǐ jiào shénme míngzì? _____
you *called* *what*   *name*

(woh)
Wǒ jiào _____.
I *called*   *(your name)*

(foo-moo)
fùmǔ
parents

(foo-cheen)
fùqin _____
father

(foo-cheen) (jee-ow)   *(meeng-zuh)*
Fùqin jiào shénme míngzì? _____
father *called* *what*   *name*

(moo-cheen)
mǔqin _____
mother

(moo-cheen)
Mǔqin jiào shénme míngzì? _____
mother *called* *what*   *name*

(ssee-ow-hi)
xiǎohái
children

Érzi and **nǚér** are also *(guh-guh)* **gēge** and *(may-may)* **mèimei**
(ur-zuh)   *(noo-ur)*   *(older) brother*   *(younger) sister*

to each other.

(ur-zuh)
érzi _____
son

(ur-zuh) (jee-ow)
Érzi jiào shénme míngzì? _____
son *called* *what*   *name*

(noo-ur)
nǚér _____
daughter

(noo-ur)
Nǚér jiào shénme míngzì? _____
daughter *called* *what*   *name*

(zoo-foo-moo)
zǔfùmǔ
grandparents

(zoo-foo)
zǔfù _____
grandfather

(zoo-foo)
Zǔfù jiào shénme míngzì? _____

(zoo-moo)
zǔmǔ _____
grandmother

(zoo-moo)
Zǔmǔ jiào shénme míngzì? _____

Now you ask —

_____

(How are you called? / What is your name?)

And answer —

_____

(My name is . . .)

- ❒ **shuǐ** *(shway)* . . . . water
- ❒ **shuǐchē** *(shway-chuh)* . . . . watermill
- ❒ **shuǐchí** *(shway-chr)* . . . . pool
- ❒ **shuǐfèn** *(shway-fuhn)* . . . . moisture
- ❒ **shuǐpíng** *(shway-peeng)* . . . . water bottle

水
shuǐ

_____
_____
_____
_____
_____

(choo-fahng)
Chúfáng
kitchen

(beeng-ssee-ahng)
bīngxiāng
refrigerator

(loo-zuh)
lúzi
stove

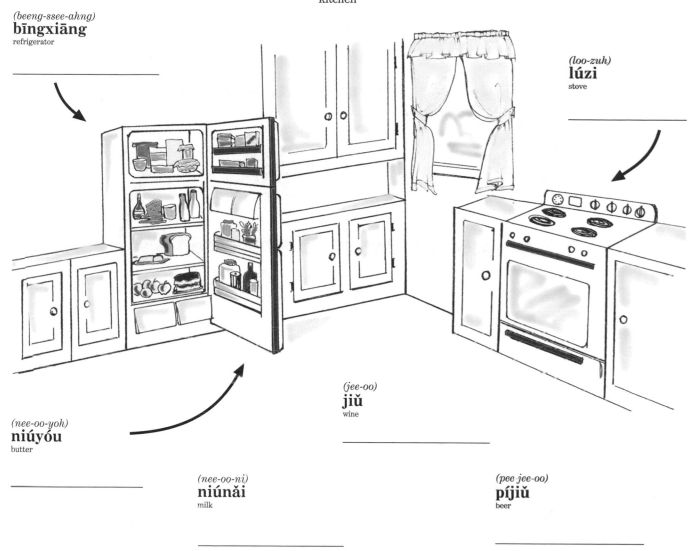

(jee-oo)
jiǔ
wine

(nee-oo-yoh)
niúyóu
butter

(nee-oo-ni)
niúnǎi
milk

(pee-jee-oo)
píjiǔ
beer

(wuhn-tee)
Answer these **wèntí** aloud.
questions

(pee-jee-oo) (zi)
Píjiǔ zài nǎr? .... **Píjiǔ zài bīngxiāng lǐ.**
beer   is   where   is   refrigerator inside
                                                   (beeng-ssee-ahng) (lee)

(nee-oo-ni)
Niúnǎi zài nǎr?   **Jiǔ zài nǎr?**   **Niúyóu zài nǎr?**   **Kuàngquán shuǐ zài nǎr?**
milk   is   where   wine is where   butter is where   mineral   water
                      (jee-oo)   *(nee-oo-yoh)*   *(kwahng-choo-ahn) (shway)*

(ssee-ahn-zi)   *(shoo)*
Xiànzài open your **shū** to the **yè** with the labels and remove the next group of labels and proceed
now   book
                        (dwong-ssee)   *(choo-fahng)*
to label all these **dōngxi** in your **chúfáng.**
                     things   kitchen

❏ **shuǐkù** *(shway-koo)* .... reservoir
❏ **shuǐshǒu** *(shway-shoh)* .... sailor
❏ **shuǐcǎi** *(shway-tsi)* .... watercolor
❏ **shuǐzāi** *(shway-zi)* .... flood
❏ **shuǐbà** *(shway-bah)* .... dam

水
shuǐ

33

(kwhy-zuh)
kuàizi
chopsticks

_____

(yahn)
yán
salt

_____

(hoo-jee-ow)
hújiāo
pepper

(jee-oo-bay)
jiŭbēi
wine glass

(bwoh-lee-bay)
bōlíbēi
glass

_____

(chah-bay)
chábēi
tea cup

_____

(bao-jihr)
bàozhĭ
newspaper

_____

(tsahn-jeen)
cānjīn
napkin

_____

(chah-zuh)
chāzi
fork

_____

(pahn-zuh)
pánzi
plate

(dow-zuh)
dāozi
knife

(tahng-chr)
tāngchí
soup spoon

_____

And more . . .

(gway-zuh)
guìzi _____
cupboard

(chah)
chá _____
tea

Chá zài năr?
tea

(gway-zuh) *(lee)*
Chá zài guìzi lĭ.
is   cupboard   inside

(kah-fay)
kāfēi _____
coffee

Kāfēi zài năr?

(mee-ahn-bao)
miànbāo _____
bread

(mee-ahn-bao) *(zi)*
Miànbāo zài năr?
bread   is   where

Don't forget to label all these things and do not forget to use every

(tsih)

opportunity to say these **cí** out loud.

(juh) *(huhn)* *(jwong-yow)*
Zhè hěn zhòngyào.
this   very   important

☐ **bīng** *(beeng)* . . . . ice
☐ **bīngbáo** *(beeng-bao)* . . . . hail
☐ **bīngxié** *(beeng-ssee-eh)* . . . . ice skates
☐ **bīnggùn** *(beeng-goon)* . . . . popsicle
☐ **bīngqílín** *(beeng-chee-leen)* . . . . ice cream

冰
bīng

_____
_____
_____
_____

(ssee-eh-ssee-eh) **xièxie**	*(shoo)* **shū**	*(gwah-lee-ahn-dow)* **guāliǎndāo**	*(nee-oo-zi-koo)* **niúzǎikù**
(dway-boo-chee) **duìbùqǐ**	*(sseen)* **xìn**	*(choo-hahn-jee)* **chúhànjì**	*(dwahn-koo)* **duǎnkù**
(yee-choo) **yīchú**	*(yoh-pee-ow)* **yóupiào**	*(shoo-zuh)* **shūzi**	*(wuhn-hwah-shahn)* **wénhuàshān**
(chwahng) **chuáng**	*(meeng-sseen-pee-ahn)* **míngxìnpiàn**	*(yoo-yee)* **yǔyī**	*(nay-koo)* **nèikù**
(juhn-toh) **zhěntóu**	*(hoo-jow)* **hùzhào**	*(sahn)* **sǎn**	*(nay-yee)* **nèiyī**
(bay-zuh) **bèizi**	*(fay-jee-pee-ow)* **fēijīpiào**	*(dah-yee)* **dàyī**	*(lee-ahn-yee-choon)* **liányīqún**
(now-jwong) **nàozhōng**	*(ssee-ahng-zuh)* **xiāngzi**	*(shoh-tao)* **shǒutào**	*(chuhn-yee)* **chènyī**
(jeeng-zuh) **jìngzi**	*(pee-bao)* **píbāo**	*(mao-zuh)* **màozi**	*(choon-zuh)* **qúnzi**
(ssee-lee-ahn-puhn) **xǐliǎnpén**	*(pee-jee-ah-zuh)* **píjiāzi**	*(ssee-yoo-eh-zuh)* **xuēzi**	*(mao-yee)* **máoyī**
(mao-jeen) **máojīn**	*(chee-ahn)* **qián**	*(ssee-eh)* **xié**	*(chuhn-choon)* **chènqún**
(mah-twong) **mǎtǒng**	*(sseen-yohng-kah)* **xìnyòngkǎ**	*(yoon-dohng-ssee-eh)* **yùndòngxié**	*(ssee-wong-jow)* **xiōngzhào**
(leen-yoo) **línyù**	*(loo-sseeng)* **lǚxíng** *(jihr-pee-ow)* **zhīpiào**	*(ssee-jwahng)* **xīzhuāng**	*(wah-zuh)* **wàzi**
(chee-ahn-bee) **qiānbǐ**	*(jow-ssee-ahng-jee)* **zhàoxiàngjī**	*(leeng-die)* **lǐngdài**	*(koo-wah)* **kùwà**
(gahng-bee) **gāngbǐ**	*(jee-ow-joo-ahn)* **jiāojuǎn**	*(chuhn-yee)* **chènyī**	*(shway-yee)* **shuìyī**
(dee-ahn-shr) **diànshì**	*(yoh-yohng-yee)* **yóyǒngyī**	*(shoh-joo-ahn)* **shǒujuàn**	*(shway-yee)* **shuìyī**
(dee-ahn-now) **diànnǎo**	*(lee-ahng-ssee-eh)* **liángxié**	*(why-tao)* **wàitào**	*(shway-pow)* **shuìpáo**
(jihr) **zhǐ**	*(tie-yahng)* **tàiyáng** *(yahn-jeeng)* **yǎnjìng**	*(koo-zuh)* **kùzi**	*(twoh-ssee-eh)* **tuōxié**
(yahn-jeeng) **yǎnjìng**	*(yah-shwah)* **yáshuā**	*(woh)* *(tswong)* *(may-gwoh)* *(lie)* **Wǒ cóng Měiguó lái.**	
(zah-jihr) **zázhì**	*(yah-gow)* **yágāo**	*(woh)* *(ssee-ahng)* *(ssee-yoo-eh-ssee)* *(jwong-wuhn)* **Wǒ xiǎng xuéxí Zhōngwén.**	
(zih-jihr-loh) **zìzhǐlǒu**	*(fay-zow)* **féizào**	*(woh)* *(jee-ow)* **Wǒ jiào _____ .**	

PLUS...

This book includes a number of other innovative features unique to the *"10 minutes a day®"* Series. At the back of this book, you will find twelve pages of flash cards. Cut them out and flip through them at least once a day.

On pages 116, 117 and 118 you will find a beverage guide and a menu guide. Don't wait until your trip to use them. Clip out the menu guide and use it tonight at the dinner table. Take them both with you the next time you dine at your favorite Chinese restaurant.

By using the special features in this book, you will be speaking Chinese before you know it.

(yee) (loo) (peeng) (ahn)
Yí lù píng ān!
safe and peaceful journey

(zwong-jee-ow)
Zōngjiào
religion

In **Zhōngguó**, there is not the wide variety of *(zwong-jee-ow)* **zōngjiào** that **wǒmen** find in *(may-gwoh)* **Měiguó.** In
religions · we · America

Zhōngguó, a person's *(zwong-jee-ow)* **zōngjiào** *(chahng-chahng)* **chángcháng** *(shr)* **shì** one of the following.
religion · generally · is

(jee-doo-jee-ow)
1. **jīdūjiào** _____
Protestant

(tee-ahn-joo-jee-ow)
2. **tiānzhǔjiào** _____
Catholic

(hway-jee-ow)
3. **huíjiào** _____
Moslem

(fwoh-jee-ow)
4. **fójiào** _____
Buddhist

This is a temple in **Zhōngguó.** ⟶

You will see several *(huhn)(dah)(duh)* **hěn dà de** temples like
very · big

this on your visit. Occasionally, for special

events or special visitors, religious services

are held in some of the temples.

(ssee-ahn-zi)
Xiànzai, let's learn how to say "I am" in *(jwong-wuhn)* **Zhōngwén:**
now

(woh)(shr)
wǒ shì _____
I · am

(woh)(zi)
wǒ zài _____
I · am (at or in)

Both these forms should look *(huhn)* **hěn** familiar. You have been using them since Step 2! Test yourself –

write each sentence on the next page for more practice. Add your own variations as well.

(how much) _____ *(chee-ahn)* **qián?**
(how much) · money / does this cost

❏	**bīngshān** *(beeng-shahn)*	iceberg	
❏	**bīngshuāng** *(beeng-shwahng)*	frost	冰
❏	**bīngtáng** *(beeng-tahng)*	rock candy	
❏	**bīngxiāng** *(beeng-ssee-ahng)*	refrigerator	*bīng*
❏	**bīngzhù** *(beeng-joo)*	icicle	

Wǒ *(shr)* **shì** *(fwoh-jee-ow)* **fójiào** *(too)* **tú.** _____
I   am   Buddhist   disciple

Wǒ *(zi)* **zài** *(jwong-gwoh)* **Zhōngguó.** _____
am (in)   China

Wǒ *(shr)* **shì** *(hway-jee-ow)* **huíjiào** *(too)* **tú.** _____
Moslem   disciple

Wǒ *(zi)* **zài** *(oh-joh)* **Ōuzhōu.** _____
am   Europe

Wǒ *(shr)* **shì** *(jee-doo-jee-ow)* **jīdūjiào** *(too)* **tú.** _____
Protestant   disciple

Wǒ *(zi)* **zài** *(loo-gwahn)* **lǚguǎn** *(lee)* **lǐ.** _____
hotel   inside

Wǒ *(shr)* **shì** *(tee-ahn-joo-jee-ow)* **tiānzhǔjiào** *(too)* **tú.** _____
Catholic   disciple

Wǒ *(zi)* **zài** *(yeen-hahng)* **yínháng** *(lee)* **lǐ.** _____
bank   inside

Wǒ *(shr)* **shì** *(yeeng-gwoh)* **Yīngguó** *(ruhn)* **rén.** _____
British   person

Wǒ *(zi)* **zài** *(choo-fahng)* **chúfáng** *(lee)* **lǐ.** _____
kitchen   inside

Wǒ *(shr)* **shì** *(jee-ah-nah-dah)* **Jiānádà** *(ruhn)* **rén.** _____
Canadian   person

Wǒ *(zi)* **zài** *(fahn-gwahn)* **fànguǎn** *(lee)* **lǐ.** _____
restaurant   inside

Wǒ *(shr)* **shì** *(may-gwoh)* **Měiguó** *(ruhn)* **rén.** _____
American   person

Wǒ *(zi)* **zài** *(fahng-zuh)* **fángzi** *(lee)* **lǐ.** _____
inside

To negate any of these statements, simply add **"bù"** *(boo)* after the subject.
not / no

Wǒ *(boo)* **bù** *(shr)* **shì** *(fwoh-jee-ow)* **fójiào** *(too)* **tú.** _____
I   not   am   Buddhist   disciple

Wǒ *(boo)* **bù** *(zi)* **zài** *(jwong-gwoh)* **Zhōngguó.** _____
not   am (in)   China

Go through and drill these sentences again but with **"bù."**

(ssee-ahn-zi) **Xiànzài**, take a piece of paper. Our *(jee-ah-teeng)* **jiātíng** from earlier had a reunion. Identify everyone
family

below by writing the *(jung-choo-eh-duh)* **zhèngquède** **Zhōngwén cí** for each *(ruhn)* **rén** – **mǔqin, shūshu,** and so on.
correct   person

Don't forget the *(goh)* **gǒu!**

- ❏ **fēi** *(fay)* . . . . to fly _____
- ❏ **fēijī** *(fay-jee)* . . . . airplane _____
- ❏ **fēijīchǎng** *(fay-jee-chahng)* . . . . airport _____
- ❏ **fēijīkù** *(fay-jee-koo)* . . . . hangar _____
- ❏ **fēiqín** *(fay-cheen)* . . . . birds

飞
fēi

You have already used two very important verbs: **wǒ** *(ssee-ahng)* **xiǎng** *(yow)* **yào** and **wǒ** *(yoh)* **yǒu.** Although you
I   would like   I   have

might be able to get by with only these verbs, let's assume you want to do better. First a quick review.

How do you say   **"I"**   in **Zhōngwén?** _____

How do you say   **"we"**   in **Zhōngwén?** _____

Compare **zhè** *(lee-ahng)* **liǎng** *(guh)* **ge** charts **hěn** carefully and **xuéxí** *(juh)* **zhè** *(lee-oo)* **liù** *(guh)* **ge** *(tsih)* **cí** now.
these two   (M)   very   learn   these six

I = **wǒ** *(woh)*		we = **wǒmen** *(woh-muhn)*	
you (sg) = **nǐ** *(nee)*		you (plural) = **nǐmen** *(nee-muhn)*	
he/she/it = **tā** *(tah)*		they = **tāmen** *(tah-muhn)*	

Not too hard, is it? Draw lines between the matching **Yīngwén** *(yeeng-wuhn)* and **Zhōngwén cí** *(jwong-wuhn)* below to see
                                                      English   Chinese

if you can keep these **cí** straight in your mind.

wǒmen *(woh-muhn)*	I
nǐmen *(nee-muhn)*	they
tā *(tah)*	you (plural)
wǒ *(woh)*	he
nǐ *(nee)*	we
tā *(tah)*	she
tāmen *(tah-muhn)*	you (singular)

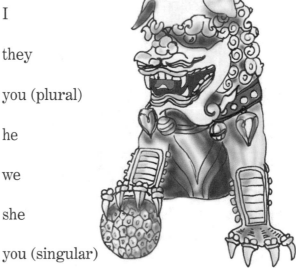

- ❏ **fēisù** *(fay-soo)* . . . . quickly
- ❏ **fēiwǔ** *(fay-woo)* . . . . to flutter
- ❏ **fēixíng** *(fay-sseeng)* . . . . to soar
- ❏ **fēixíngyuán** *(fay-sseeng-yoo-ahn)* . . . . pilot
- ❏ **fēiyú** *(fay-yoo)* . . . . flying fish

fēi

_____
_____
_____
_____
_____

(ssee-ahn-zi)
Xiànzài close this **shū** and write out both columns of the above exercise on a piece of **zhǐ** *(jihr)* and do
paper

it again. How did **nǐ** do? **Hǎo** *(how)* or **bù hǎo?** *(boo)(how)* **Mǎmǎhūhū?** *(mah-mah-hoo-hoo)* **Xiànzài** that **nǐ** *(nee)* know these **cí, nǐ** can
good not good so so you

say almost anything in **Zhōngwén** with one basic formula: the "plug-in" formula.

To demonstrate, let's take **liù** *(lee-oo)* **ge** basic and practical verbs and see how the "plug-in" formula
six (M)

works. Write the verbs in the blanks after **nǐ** *(nee)* have practiced saying them out loud many times.
you

(lie)
lái _____
to come

(choo)
qù *qù, qù, qù, qù, qù, qù*
to go to

(ssee-ahng) (yow)
xiǎng yào _____
would like

(ssee-yoo-eh-ssee)
xuéxí _____
to learn

(yoh)
yǒu _____
to have

(ssee-oo-yow)
xūyào _____
to need

Besides the familiar words already circled, can **nǐ** find the above verbs in the puzzle below?

When **nǐ** find them, write them in the blanks to the right.

P	D	O	Q	Ù	A	I	D	E	À	X
A	U	C	N	P	C	N	Ǎ	R	E	U
E	Ō	X	Ū	Y	À	O	J	J	Í	É
W	S	L	S	J	E	E	U	O	I	X
E	H	Á	E	Ǐ	T	Z	U	Y	E	Í
J	A	I	I	I	E	Ó	M	Ǒ	W	E
D	O	N	Z	H	X	B	D	U	I	F
X	I	Ǎ	N	G	Y	À	O	Y	Ǐ	È

1. _____

2. _____

3. _____

4. _____

5. _____

6. _____

☐ **shū** *(shoo)* .... book
☐ **shūbāo** *(shoo-bao)* .... bookbag
☐ **shūchú** *(shoo-choo)* .... bookcase
☐ **shūjià** *(shoo-jee-ah)* .... bookshelf
☐ **shūqiān** *(shoo-chee-ahn)* .... bookmark

书
shū

_____
_____
_____
_____

40

Study the following patterns carefully.

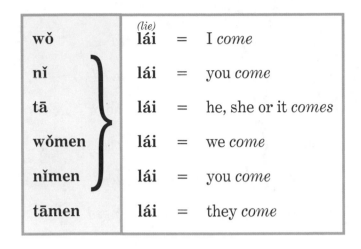

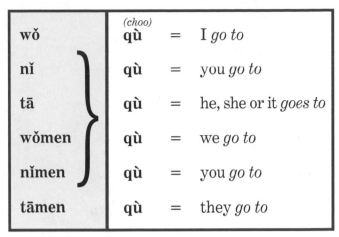

wǒ	*(lie)* **lái**	=	I *come*
nǐ	**lái**	=	you *come*
tā	**lái**	=	he, she or it *comes*
wǒmen	**lái**	=	we *come*
nǐmen	**lái**	=	you *come*
tāmen	**lái**	=	they *come*

wǒ	*(choo)* **qù**	=	I *go to*
nǐ	**qù**	=	you *go to*
tā	**qù**	=	he, she or it *goes to*
wǒmen	**qù**	=	we *go to*
nǐmen	**qù**	=	you *go to*
tāmen	**qù**	=	they *go to*

Note: • Regardless of the subject of the sentence in Chinese (I, we, you, he, she, it, they), the same verb form is used. Verbs remain the same in Chinese – they do not have different endings. What could be easier?

Notice that *(muhn)* **"men"** is added to a word to indicate more than one person.

wǒ	=	I	*(woh-muhn)* **wǒmen**	=	we
(nee) **nǐ**	=	you (singular)	*(nee-muhn)* **nǐmen**	=	you (plural as in "you all")
tā	=	he, she or it	*(tah-muhn)* **tāmen**	=	they

Note: • Unlike English, the same word is used for he, she and it: **tā.**

he *learns* she *learns* it *learns*	*(ssee-yoo-eh-ssee)* **tā xuéxí** _____

he *would like* she *would like* it *would like*	*(ssee-ahng) (yow)* **tā xiǎng yào** _____

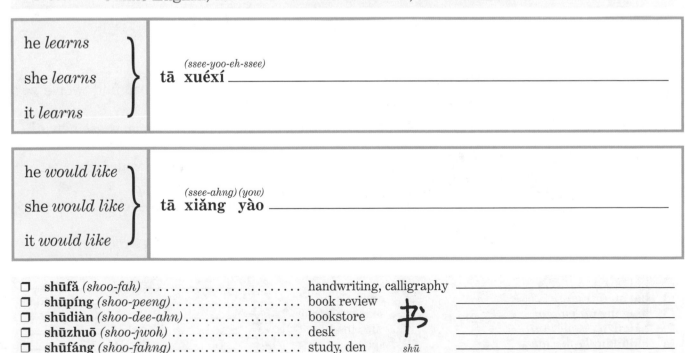

❏ **shūfǎ** *(shoo-fah)* . . . . handwriting, calligraphy _____
❏ **shūpíng** *(shoo-peeng)* . . . . book review
❏ **shūdiàn** *(shoo-dee-ahn)* . . . . bookstore
❏ **shūzhuō** *(shoo-jwoh)* . . . . desk
❏ **shūfáng** *(shoo-fahng)* . . . . study, den   *shū*

Here's your next group!

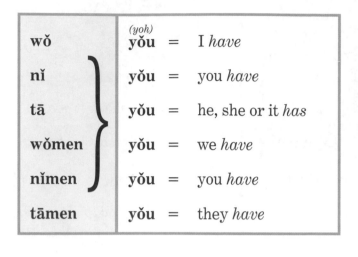

	(yoh)	
wǒ	yǒu	= I *have*
nǐ	yǒu	= you *have*
tā	yǒu	= he, she or it *has*
wǒmen	yǒu	= we *have*
nǐmen	yǒu	= you *have*
tāmen	yǒu	= they *have*

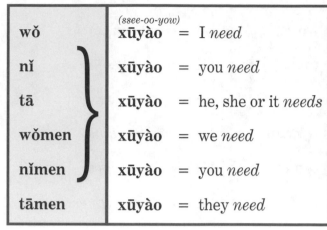

	(ssee-oo-yow)	
wǒ	xūyào	= I *need*
nǐ	xūyào	= you *need*
tā	xūyào	= he, she or it *needs*
wǒmen	xūyào	= we *need*
nǐmen	xūyào	= you *need*
tāmen	xūyào	= they *need*

In **Zhōngwén**, **dòngcí** *(dwong-tsih)* — verbs — are easy to learn. **Zhèr** *(juhr)* here **yǒu** *(yoh)* **liù** *(lee-oo)* six **ge** **dòngcí.** *(dwong-tsih)* verbs.

(jee-ow)
jiào _____
to be called, named

(shwoh)
shuō _____
to speak

(jee-ow)
jiào _____
to order

(my)
mǎi _____
to buy

(joo)
zhù _____
to live, reside

(teeng-lee-oo)
tíngliú _____
to stay

Notice that the verb for "to order" and "to be called" is one and the same: **Jiào.** *(jee-ow)* Don't panic or give up. Just think of it as one less word to learn. Be sure to write out all these verbs and sentences and then try to use them in sentences of your own.

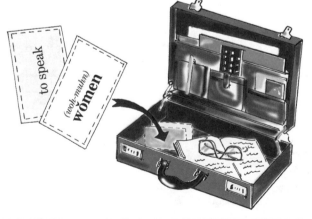

At the back of this **shū,** *(shoo)* **nǐ** *(nee)* will find twelve **yè** *(yeh)* of flash cards to help you learn these new **cí.** *(tsih)* Cut them out; carry them in your briefcase, purse, pocket **huòzhě** *(hwoh-juh)* or knapsack; and review them whenever **nǐ** have a free moment.

❐ **hǎi** *(hi)*	sea	
❐ **hǎi àn** *(hi)(ahn)*	coast	
❐ **hǎigǎng** *(hi-gahng)*	seaport, harbor	海 _____
❐ **hǎiguān** *(hi-gwahn)*	customs	_____
❐ **hǎimián** *(hi-mee-ahn)*	sponge	*hǎi* _____

42

(ssee-ahn-zi)
Xiànzài, it is your turn to practice what **nǐ** *(nee)* have learned. Fill in the following blanks with the

correct form of the **dòngcí**. *(dwong-tsih)* Each time **nǐ** write out the sentence, be sure to say it aloud.
verb

(lie)
lái
to come

(ssee-yoo-eh-ssee)
xuéxi
to learn

(tswong) (may-gwoh)
Wǒ cóng Měiguó _____ .
from   America

Wǒ _____ **Zhōngwén.** *(jwong-wuhn)*

(duh-gwoh)
Nǐ cóng Déguó _____ .
Germany

Nǐ _____ **Yīngwén.** *(yeeng-wuhn)*
English

(fah-gwoh)
Tā cóng Fǎguó *lái/* _____ .
France

Tā _____ **Zhōngwén.**

(yeeng-gwoh)
Wǒmen cóng Yīngguó _____ .
England

Wǒmen _____ **Yīngwén.**

Tāmen cóng Zhōngguó _____ .

Tāmen _____ **Zhōngwén.**

(choo)
qù
to go to

(yoh)
yǒu
to have

Wǒ _____ **Déguó.** *(duh-gwoh)*
Germany

Wǒ _____ **wǔ yuán.** *(woo)*
five   yuan

Nǐ _____ **Fǎguó.** *(fah-gwoh)*
France

Nǐ _____ **liù yuán.** *(lee-oo)*
six

Tā *qù/* _____ **Yìdàlì.** *(yee-dah-lee)*
Italy

Tā _____ **bā yuán.**

Wǒmen _____ **Hélán.** *(huh-lahn)*
Netherlands

Wǒmen _____ **shí yuán.** *(shr)*
ten

Tāmen _____ **Zhōngguó.**

Tāmen _____ **sān yuán.**

(ssee-ahng) (yow)
xiǎng yào
would like

(ssee-oo-yow)
xūyào
to need

Wǒ _____ **yì bēi jiǔ.** *(yee) (bay) (jee-oo)*
one   cup/glass wine

Wǒ _____ **yì jiān fángjiān.** *(yee) (jee-ahn)(fahng-jee-ahn)*
one   (M)   room

Nǐ _____ **yì bēi chá.** *(chah)*
cup   tea

Nǐ *xūyào/* _____ **yì jiān fángjiān.** *(yee) (jee-ahn)(fahng-jee-ahn)*

Tā _____ **yì bēi shuǐ.** *(shway)*
(M)   water

Tā _____ **yì jiān fángjiān.**

Wǒmen _____ **yì bēi júzishuǐ.** *(joo-zuh-shway)*
(M)   orange juice

Wǒmen _____ **yì jiān fángjiān.**

Tāmen _____ **yì bēi píjiǔ.** *(pee-jee-oo)*
(M)   beer

Tāmen _____ **yì jiān fángjiān.**

❏ **hǎitān** *(hi-tahn)* . . . . beach
❏ **hǎiwài** *(hi-why)* . . . . overseas
❏ **hǎiwān** *(hi-wahn)* . . . . bay, gulf
❏ **hǎiwèi** *(hi-way)* . . . . seafood
❏ **hǎiyáng** *(hi-yahng)* . . . . ocean

海
hǎi

_____
_____
_____
_____
_____

43

Now take a break, walk around the room, take a deep breath and do the next *(lee-oo)* *(dwong-tsih)* **liù ge dòngcí.**
six   verbs

(jee-ow)
jiào
to be called / named

Wǒ jiào/ _____ *(yoo-eh-hahn)* **Yuēhàn.**

Nǐ _____ *(mah-lee)* **Mǎlì.**

Tā _____ *(jee-ahn)* **Jiàn.**

Wǒmen _____ Yuēhàn, Mǎlì *(huh)* hé Jiàn.
and

Tāmen _____ Yuēhàn, Mǎlì hé Jiàn.

Wǒ jiào Mǎlì.

(my)
mǎi
to buy

Wǒ _____ *(yee)* yí liàng *(zih-sseeng-chuh)* **zìxíngchē.**
one (M) bicycle

Nǐ _____ yí pán *(suh-lah)* **sèlā.**
(M) salad

Tā _____ *(jahng)* yì zhāng *(hwahr)* **huàr.**
(M) picture

Wǒmen _____ *(jwong)* yí ge **zhōng.**
(M) clock

(tah-muhn) Tāmen _____ *(tie-dung)* yí ge **táidēng.**
table lamp

(shwoh)
shuō
to speak

Wǒ _____ **Zhōngwén.**

Nǐ shuō/ _____ *(fah-wuhn)* **Fǎwén.**
French

Tā _____ *(yeeng-wuhn)* **Yīngwén.**
English

Wǒmen _____ *(ree-wuhn)* **Rìwén.**
Japanese

(nee-muhn) Nǐmen _____ *(duh-wuhn)* **Déwén.**
German

Nín zǎo!

(joo)
zhù
to live / reside

Wǒ _____ *(zi)* zài **Zhōngguó.**
in

Nǐ _____ zài *(fah-gwoh)* **Fǎguó.**
France

Tā _____ zài *(may-gwoh)* **Měiguó.**

(woh-muhn) Wǒmen _____ zài *(oh-joh)* **Ōuzhōu.**
Europe

Nǐmen zhù/ _____ zài *(duh-gwoh)* **Déguó.**
Germany

(jee-ow)
jiào
to order

Wǒ _____ *(bay)* *(shway)* yì bēi **shuǐ.**
one glass water

Nǐ _____ *(jee-oo)* yì bēi **jiǔ.**
(M) wine

Tā jiào/ _____ *(joo-zuh-shway)* yì bēi **júzishuǐ.**
orange juice

Wǒmen _____ yì bēi **chá.**

Tāmen _____ *(nee-oo-ni)* yì bēi **niúnǎi.**
milk

(teeng-lee-oo)
tíngliú
to stay

Wǒ _____ *(tee-ahn)* wǔ **tiān.**
days

Nǐ _____ sān **tiān.**

Tā _____ liǎng **tiān.**

Wǒmen _____ liù **tiān.**

Tāmen _____ bā **tiān.**

- ❑ **fàn** *(fahn)* .... meal
- ❑ **fànguǎn** *(fahn-gwahn)* .... restaurant
- ❑ **wǎnfàn** *(wahn-fahn)* .... supper
- ❑ **wǔfàn** *(woo-fahn)* .... lunch
- ❑ **zǎofàn** *(zow-fahn)* .... breakfast

饭
fàn

_____
_____
_____
_____
_____

44

Shì, *(shr)* it is hard to get used to all those **xīn** *(sseen)* **cí** *(tsih)*. Just keep practicing and before **nǐ** know it, **nǐ** will be using them naturally. **Xiànzài** *(ssee-ahn-zi)* is a perfect time to turn to the back of this **shū,** clip out your verb flash cards and start flashing. Don't skip over your free **cí** either. Check them off in the box provided as **nǐ xuéxí** *(ssee-yoo-eh-ssee)* each one. See if **nǐ** can fill in the blanks below. The answers **zài** *(zi)* at the bottom of **zhèi** *(juh-ay)* **yè** *(yeh)*.

1. _____
(I speak Chinese.)

2. _____
(We learn Chinese.)

3. _____
(She needs ten yuan.)

4. _____
(He comes from Canada.)

5. _____
(They live in China.)

6. _____
(You buy a book.)

In the following Steps, **nǐ** will be introduced to more verbs and **nǐ** should drill them in exactly the same way as **nǐ** did in this section. Look up **xīn** *(sseen)* **cí** *(tsih)* in your **cídiǎn** *(tsih-dee-ahn)* and make up your own sentences. Try out your **xīn** *(sseen)* **cí** for that's how you make them yours to use on your holiday. Remember, the more **nǐ** practice **xiànzài,** the more enjoyable your trip will be. **Zhù** *(joo)* **nǐ** *(nee)* **shùnlì!** *(shoon-lee)*

(jee) (dee-ahn) (luh)
Jǐ diǎn le?
what time is it (how many hours is it)

Nǐ know **zěnme** *(zuhn-muh)* how to tell the **tiān** *(tee-ahn)* days of the **xīngqī** *(sseeng-chee)* week and the **yuè** *(yoo-eh)* months of the **nián,** *(nee-ahn)* year so **xiànzài** let's learn to tell time. Punctuality **zài Zhōngguó** *(zi)* in is **hěn zhòngyào,** *(huhn) (jwong-yow)* important not to mention the need to catch **huǒchē** *(hwoh-chuh)* trains and arrive on time. **Zhèr** *(juhr)* here **shì** *(shr)* are the "basics." Notice that **le** *(luh)* is often used to complete sentences in **Zhōngwén.**

What time is it?	=	**Jǐ diǎn le?** *(jee) (dee-ahn) (luh)* _____
time	=	**shíjiān** *(shr-jee-ahn)* _____
o'clock	=	**diǎn** *(dee-ahn)* _____
minute	=	**fēn** *(fuhn)* _____
a quarter (15 minutes)	=	**shíwǔ fēn** *(shr-woo) (fuhn)* _____
hour	=	**xiǎoshí** *(ssee-ow-shr)* _____
half past	=	**bàn** *(bahn)* _____
noon	=	**zhōngwǔ** *(jwong-woo)* _____
midnight	=	**wǔyè** *(woo-yeh)* _____

Xiànzài quiz yourself. Fill in the missing letters below.

midnight = | w | | y | |

half past = | b | | |

minute = | f | | |

a quarter = | s | h | | ǔ | × | f | n |

time = | | | í | j | i | | |

o'clock = | d | i | |

and finally　　when = | s | | | | e | × | s | | | | | u |

❏ **fáng** *(fahng)*	room, apartment	_____
❏ **fángdōng** *(fahng-dwong)*	landlord	_____
❏ **fángkè** *(fahng-kuh)*	tenant	房
❏ **fángzi** *(fahng-zuh)*	house	_____
❏ **shuìfáng** *(shwei-fahng)*	bedroom	*fáng*

Xiànzài, zěnme *(zuhn-muh)* (how) are these **cí** *(tsih)* (words) used? Study the examples below. When **nǐ** think it through, it really is not too difficult. Don't forget that **liǎng** *(lee-ahng)* means "two" in **Zhōngwén** as does **èr** *(ur)*.

Wǔ diǎn. *(woo)* *(dee-ahn)*
five o'clock

`5:00`

Wǔ diǎn. Wǔ diǎn. Wǔ diǎn.

Wǔ diǎn shí fēn. *(shr)* *(fuhn)*
ten minutes

`5:10`

_____

Wǔ diǎn shíwǔ fēn. *(shr-woo)*

`5:15`

_____

Wǔ diǎn èrshí fēn. *(ur-shr)*

`5:20`

_____

Wǔ diǎn bàn. *(bahn)*
(+) half

`5:30`

_____

Wǔ diǎn sìshí fēn. *(sih-shr)*

`5:40`

_____

Wǔ diǎn sìshíwǔ fēn. *(sih-shr-woo)*

`5:45`

_____

Wǔ diǎn wǔshí fēn. *(woo-shr)*

`5:50`

_____

Liù diǎn. *(lee-oo)*
o'clock

`6:00`

_____

See how **zhòngyào** *(jwong-yow)* (important) it is to learn the **shùzì** (numbers)? Answer the following **wèntí** *(wuhn-tee)* (questions) based on the **zhōng** *(jwong)* (clocks) below. **Jǐ diǎn le?** *(jee)* *(luh)*

1. `8:00` _____

2. `7:15` _____

3. `4:30` _____

4. `9:20` _____

When **nǐ** answer a *(shr-jee-ahn)* **shíjiān** time *(wuhn-tee)* **wèntí,** question it is not necessary to say **"fēn"** *(fuhn)* after the number of minutes

if the number is larger than ten.

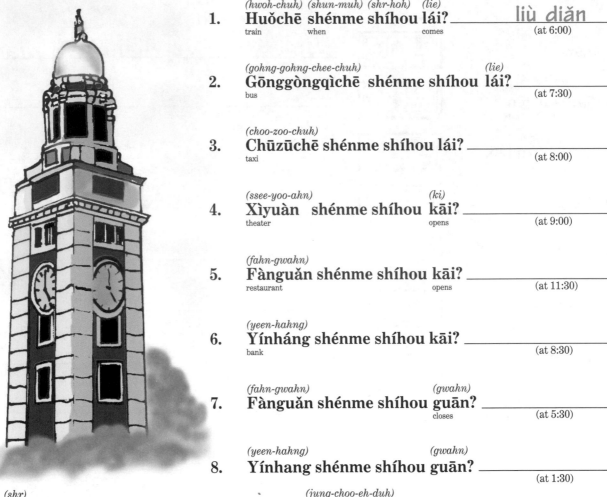

1. *(hwoh-chuh)* **Huǒchē** train *(shun-muh)* **shénme** when *(shr-hoh)* **shíhou** *(lie)* **lái?** comes _____ liù diǎn (at 6:00)

2. *(gohng-gohng-chee-chuh)* **Gōnggòngqìchē** bus **shénme shíhou** *(lie)* **lái?** _____ (at 7:30)

3. *(choo-zoo-chuh)* **Chūzūchē** taxi **shénme shíhou lái?** _____ (at 8:00)

4. *(ssee-yoo-ahn)* **Xìyuàn** theater **shénme shíhou** *(ki)* **kāi?** opens _____ (at 9:00)

5. *(fahn-gwahn)* **Fànguǎn** restaurant **shénme shíhou kāi?** opens _____ (at 11:30)

6. *(yeen-hahng)* **Yínháng** bank **shénme shíhou kāi?** _____ (at 8:30)

7. *(fahn-gwahn)* **Fànguǎn** restaurant **shénme shíhou** *(gwahn)* **guān?** closes _____ (at 5:30)

8. *(yeen-hahng)* **Yínhang** bank **shénme shíhou** *(gwahn)* **guān?** _____ (at 1:30)

(juhr) **Zhèr** here *(shr)* **shì** is **yí ge** quick quiz. Fill in the blanks with *(jung-choo-eh-duh)* **zhèngquède** correct **shùzì.** The answers **zài** *(ssee-ah-bee-ahn)* **xiàbiān.** below

9. *(yee)* **Yì** one *(fuhn)* **fēn** minute *(yoh)* **yǒu** has _____ (?) *(mee-ow)* **miǎo.** seconds

10. **Yí ge** (M) *(ssee-ow-shr)* **xiǎoshí** hour **yǒu** has _____ (?) **fēn.** minutes

11. **Yí ge** *(sseeng-chee)* **xīngqī** week **yǒu** _____ (?) **tiān.** days

12. **Yì** *(nee-ahn)* **nián** year **yǒu** _____ (?) **ge yuè.** *(yoo-eh)* months

12. **Yì nián yǒu** _____ (?) **ge** *(sseeng-chee)* **xīngqī.** week

14. **Yì nián yǒu** _____ (?) **tiān.**

ANSWERS

8. yī diǎn bàn	1. liù diǎn
9. liùshí	2. qī diǎn bàn
10. liùshí	3. bā diǎn
11. qī	4. jiǔ diǎn
12. shíèr	5. shíyī diǎn bàn
13. wǔshíèr	6. bā diǎn bàn
14. sānbǎi liùshíwǔ	7. wǔ diǎn bàn

48

Do **nǐ** remember your greetings from earlier? It is a good time to review them as they will

always be **hěn** *(huhn)* **zhòngyào.** *(jwong-yow)*
very   important

Shàngwǔ *(shahng-woo)* **bā diǎn** **rénmen** *(ruhn-muhn)* **shuō,** *(shwoh)* "**Nín** *(neen)* **zǎo!**" *(zow)*
morning   eight   people   say   good morning

Rénmen shuō *(shwoh)* **shénme?** *(shun-muh)* _____ *Nín zǎo! Nín zǎo! Nín zǎo!* _____
what

Xiàwǔ *(ssee-ah-woo)* **yì diǎn rénmen** **shuō,** *(shwoh)* "**Nǐ** *(nee)* **hǎo** *(how)* **ma?**"
afternoon   how are you

Rénmen shuō *(ruhn-muhn)* **shénme?** _____

Xiàwǔ *(ssee-ah-woo)* **sān diǎn rénmen** **chángcháng** *(chahng-chahng)* **shuō,** "**Míngtiān** *(meeng-tee-ahn)* **jiàn.**" *(jee-ahn)*
afternoon   often   see you tomorrow

Rénmen shuō *(ruhn-muhn)* **shénme?** _____

Wǎnshàng *(wahng-shahng)* **shí** *(shr)* **diǎn rénmen shuō,** "**Wǎn** *(wahn)* **ān!**" *(ahn)*
evening   good night

Rénmen shuō *(ruhn-muhn)* **shénme?** _____

Remember the meaning of **Zhōngwén cí** varies depending upon the tone used. Look at the two

words **mǎi** *(my)* and **mài.** *(my)* Notice the differences in the meanings below and then practice using the
to buy   to sell

tones by saying each **cí** out loud. Review the many words **nǐ** have learned and make a list similar

to the one below of those which are pronounced the same except for the tone.

		(bah)		*(tee)*		*(mah)*	
Tone 1:	▬	**bā** = scar		**tī** = ladder		**mā** = mother	
Tone 2:	╱	**bá** = to pull up		**tí** = to lift		**má** = hemp	
Tone 3:	⌵	**bǎ** = measure word		**tǐ** = body		**mǎ** = horse	
Tone 4:	╲	**bà** = father		**tì** = tears		**mà** = curse	

Don't worry. First learn your vocabulary and then play with the tones. Soon you will feel

comfortable with the different pronunciations, although it seems a bit overwhelming at first.

❑ **zhǐ** *(jihr)*........................ paper _____
❑ **zhǐbì** *(jihr-bee)*........................ paper currency _____
❑ **bàozhǐ** *(bao-jihr)*........................ newspaper 纸 _____
❑ **wèishēngzhǐ** *(way-shuhng-jihr)* .... toilet paper *zhǐ* _____
❑ **zìzhǐlǒu** *(zuh-jihr-loh)*................ wastepaper basket _____

49

Zhèr shì *(lee-ahng)* **liǎng ge** *(sseen)* **xīn** *(dwong-tsih)* **dòngcí** for Step 13.

(chr) — two — (M) — new — verbs

(chr)
chī _____
to eat

(huh)
hē
to drink

(chr)
chī
to eat

(huh)
hē
to drink

Wǒ _____ *(shway-gwoh)* **shuǐguǒ.**
fresh fruit

Nǐ _____ *(zow-fahn)* **zǎofàn.**
breakfast

Tā _____ *(yoo)* **yú.**
fish

Wǒmen _____ *(roh)* **ròu.**
meat

(nee-muhn)
Nǐmen _____ *(jee-dahn)* **jīdàn.**
eggs

Tāmen _____ *(joo-roh)* **zhūròu.**
pork

Wǒ _____ *(nee-oo-ni)* **niúnǎi.**
milk

Nǐ _hē/_ _____ *(joo-zuh-shway)* **júzishuǐ.**
orange juice

Tā _____ **jiǔ.**
wine

(woh-muhn)
Wǒmen _____ **chá.**

Nǐmen _____ **kāfēi.**

Tāmen _____ *(kwahng-choo-ahn)* **kuàngquán** *(shway)* **shuǐ.**
mineral — water

Remember that "**c**" as in "**cí**" *(tsih)* is pronounced like the "ts" in "its." Practice this sound with the following words:

(tsuh-swoh) **cèsuǒ,** lavatory *(tswong)* **cóng,** from *(tsahn-jeen)* **cānjīn,** napkin *(tsow)* **cǎo,** grass *(tsi)* **cài,** vegetables *(tsi-dahn)* **càidān,** menu *(tsahn-chuh)* **cānchē.** dining car

❏ **huǒ** *(hwoh)* .... fire, flame _____
❏ **huǒchái** *(hwoh-chi)* .... match _____
❏ **huǒchē** *(hwoh-chuh)* .... train _____
❏ **huǒshān** *(hwoh-shahn)* .... volcano _____
❏ **huǒjiàn** *(hwoh-jee-ahn)* .... rocket _____

火

huǒ

Nǐ have learned a lot of material in the last few steps and that means it is time to quiz yourself. Don't panic, this is just for you and no one else needs to know how **nǐ** did. Remember, this is a chance to review, find out what **nǐ** remember and what **nǐ** need to spend more time on. After **nǐ** have finished, check your answers in the glossary at the back of this book. Circle the **correct** answers.

kāfēi	tea	coffee	**jiātíng**	seven	family
bù	yes	no	**xiǎohái**	children	grandfather
gūgu	aunt	uncle	**niúnǎi**	butter	milk
yánsè	house	color	**yán**	pepper	salt
xuéxí	to drink	to learn	**shàngbiān**	under	over
yèlǐ	morning	night	**yīshēng**	man	doctor
xīngqīwǔ	Friday	Tuesday	**qīyuè**	June	July
shuō	to live	to speak	**zōngjiào**	kitchen	religion
xiàtiān	summer	winter	**wǒ yǒu**	I would like	I have
qián	money	page	**mǎi**	to order	to buy
shí	nine	ten	**míngtiān**	yesterday	tomorrow
miànbāo	spoon	bread	**huáng**	good	yellow

(niúnǎi — milk is circled)

(nee) (how) (mah)
Nǐ hǎo ma? <u>What time is it?</u> <u>How are you?</u> Well, how are you after this quiz?

- ❏ **huā/huār** *(hwah/hwahr)* .... flower
- ❏ **huā duǒ** *(hwah)(dwoh)* .... blossom
- ❏ **huā píng** *(hwah)(peeng)* .... flower vase
- ❏ **huā quān** *(hwah)(chwahn)* .... wreath
- ❏ **huā shù** *(hwah)(shoo)* .... bouquet

花
huā

_____
_____
_____
_____
_____

14

Dōng - Xī, Běi - Nán
(dwong) east — *(ssee)* west — *(bay)* north — *(nahn)* south

While in **Zhōngguó, nǐ** *(nee)* you will no doubt use a **dìtú** *(dee-too)* map. Study the direction words **xiàbiān** *(ssee-ah-bee-ahn)* below until **nǐ** are familiar with them and can recognize them on a **dìtú** *(dee-too)* map.

dōng *(dwong)* east _____

xī *(ssee)* west _____

běi *(bay)* north _____

nán *(nahn)* south _____

Be prepared – because on your **dìtú** *(dee-too)* map and when you are given directions in **Zhōngguó,** your directions will be given as "**dōngnán**" *(east-south)* and "**xīběi,**" *(ssee-bay)* *(west-north)* rather than "southeast" and "northwest."

Also notice how the direction words are combined with the word **biān** *(bee-ahn)* side and **fāng** *(fahng)* direction below.

běibiān *(bay-bee-ahn)* = North _____

nánbiān *(nahn-bee-ahn)* = South _____

dōngbiān *(dwong-bee-ahn)* = East _____

xībiān *(ssee-bee-ahn)* = West _____

běifāng *(bay-fahng)* = northern _____

nánfāng *(nahn-fahng)* = southern ___*nánfāng*___

dōngfāng *(dwong-fahng)* = eastern _____

xīfāng *(ssee-fahng)* = western _____

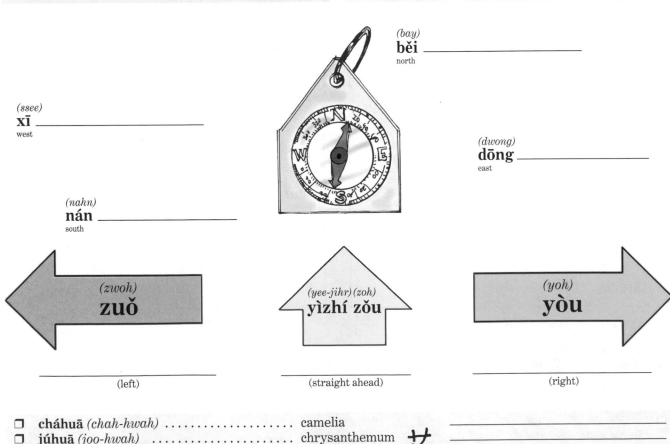

běi *(bay)* north _____

xī *(ssee)* west _____

dōng *(dwong)* east _____

nán *(nahn)* south _____

zuǒ *(zwoh)*

yìzhí zǒu *(yee-jihr) (zoh)*

yòu *(yoh)*

_____ (left)

_____ (straight ahead)

_____ (right)

❐ **cháhuā** *(chah-hwah)* .... camelia

❐ **júhuā** *(joo-hwah)* .... chrysanthemum

❐ **lánhuā** *(lahn-hwah)* .... orchid

❐ **méiguìhuā** *(may-gway-hwah)* .... rose

❐ **xuěhuā** *(ssee-oo-eh-hwah)* .... snowflake

花 *huā*

_____
_____
_____
_____
_____

These **cí** can go a long way. Say them aloud each time you write them in the blanks below.

(cheeng)
qǐng _____
please

(ssee-eh-ssee-eh) or *(shee-shee)*
xièxie _____
thank you

(dway-boo-chee) *(cheeng-wuhn)*
duìbùqǐ / qǐngwèn _____
excuse me   excuse me, may I ask

(boo) *(ssee-eh)*
bú xiè _____
you're welcome

(juhr) *(shr)*   *(huhn)* *(dee-ahn-sseeng-duh)* *(dway-hwah)*
Zhèr shì liǎng ge hěn diǎnxíngde duìhuà for someone who is trying to find something.
two   very   typical   conversations

Write them out in the blanks below.

         (cheeng-wuhn)   *(loo-gwahn)*   *(zi)*
Zhāng Sān: **Qǐngwèn, Běijīng Lǚguǎn zài nǎr?**
           excuse me, may I ask   is

_____

       (yee-jihr) *(zoh)* *(zi)* *(zwoh-bee-ahn)*
Lǐ Sì: **Yìzhí zǒu zài zuǒbiān.**
              on   left-hand side

_____

               (loo-gwahn)
        Nà shì Běijīng Lǚguǎn.

_____

                            (bwoh-woo-gwahn)
Zhāng Sān: **Qǐngwèn, Zhōngguó Bówùguǎn zài nǎr?**
           excuse me, may I ask   museum

_____

         (juhr) *(yoh)* *(jwahn)* *(yee-jihr)* *(zoh)*
Lǐ Sì: **Zài zhèr yòu zhuǎn, yìzhí zǒu,**
        from here right turn   straight ahead

_____

             (bwoh-woo-gwahn)   *(yoh-bee-ahn)*
        Zhōngguó Bówùguǎn zài yòubiān.
                               right side

_____

☐ **zì** *(zih)*. . . . . Chinese character _____
☐ **zìdiǎn** *(zih-dee-ahn)*. . . . . character dictionary _____
☐ **zìtiáo** *(zih-tee-ow)*. . . . . note   字 _____
☐ **zìmǔ** *(zih-moo)* . . . . letters of alphabet _____
☐ **zìmù** *(zih-moo)* . . . . subtitles   *zì* _____

Are **nǐ** lost? There is no need to be lost if **nǐ xuéxí** *(ssee-yoo-eh-ssee)* **le** the basic direction **cí.** Do not try to
learned

memorize these **duìhuà** *(dway-hwah)* because **nǐ** will never be looking for precisely these places. One day, **nǐ**
conversations

might need to ask for directions to "**Tàiyáng Fànguǎn**" *(tie-yahng) (lee-shr)* or " **Lìshǐ Bówùguǎn.**" *(bwoh-woo-gwahn)* Learn the
sun restaurant history

key direction **cí** and be sure **nǐ** can find your destination. **Nǐ** may want to buy a guidebook to

start planning which places **nǐ** would like to visit. Practice asking directions to these special

places. What if the person responding to your **wèntí** *(wuhn-tee)* answers too quickly for **nǐ** to understand
question

the entire reply? Practice saying,

(dway-boo-chee)		*(boo)*	*(dwong)*	*(cheeng)*	*(zi)*	*(shwoh)*	*(yee-bee-ahn)*	*(ssee-eh-ssee-eh)*
Duìbùqǐ.	**Wǒ**	**bù**	**dǒng.**	**Qǐng**	**zài**	**shuō**	**yíbiàn.**	**Xièxie.**
excuse me		*not*	*understand*	*please*	*repeat*			

Break it into pieces, say it again and again, and then write it out below.

_____

(Excuse me. I do not understand. Please repeat. Thank you.)

Shì, it is difficult at first but don't give up! **Shénme shíhou** *(shr-hoh)* the directions are repeated, **nǐ** will be
yes   *when*

able to understand if **nǐ** have learned the key **cí.** Let's review by writing them in the blanks below.

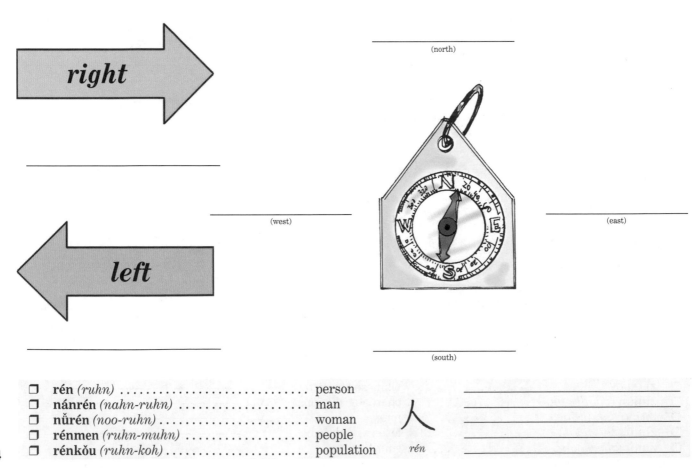

right

left

_____
(north)

_____
(west)

_____
(east)

_____
(south)

☐ **rén** *(ruhn)* . . . . person   _____
☐ **nánrén** *(nahn-ruhn)* . . . . man   _____
☐ **nǚrén** *(noo-ruhn)* . . . . woman   _____
☐ **rénmen** *(ruhn-muhn)* . . . . people   _____
☐ **rénkǒu** *(ruhn-koh)* . . . . population   _____

人
rén

(juhr) *(sseen)* *(dwong-tsih)*
Zhèr shì jǐ ge xīn dòngcí.
some (M) new verbs

(shwoh)
shuō _____
to say

(my)
mài màì, màì, màì, màì, màì
to sell

(dwong)
dǒng _____
to understand

(zi) *(shwoh)* *(yee-bee-ahn)*
zài shuō yíbiàn _____
to repeat, say once again

Did you notice that the only difference between the **dòngcí** "**mài**" **hé** "**mǎi**" is the tone?
(dwong-tsih) *(my)* *(huh)* *(my)*
verbs to sell and to buy

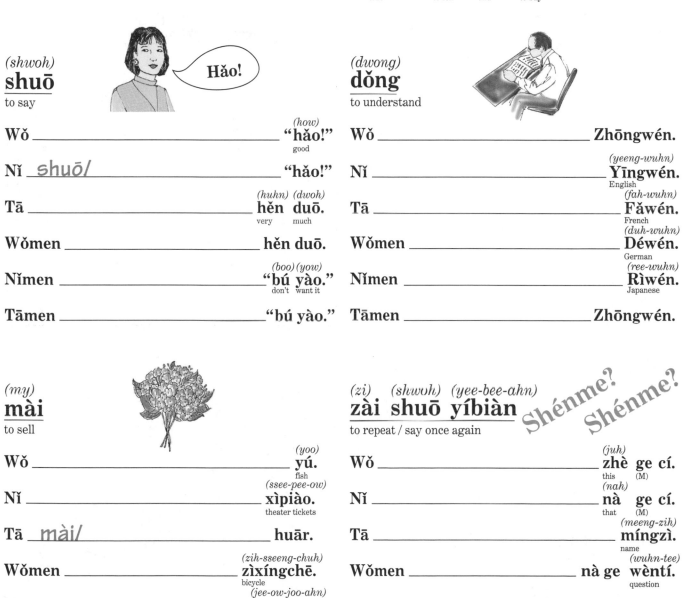

(shwoh)
shuō
to say

Wǒ	_____	"hǎo!"	*(how)* good
Nǐ	_shuō/_____	"hǎo!"	
Tā	_____	hěn duō.	*(huhn) (dwoh)* very much
Wǒmen	_____	hěn duō.	
Nǐmen	_____	"bú yào."	*(boo) (yow)* don't want it
Tāmen	_____	"bú yào."	

(dwong)
dǒng
to understand

Wǒ	_____	Zhōngwén.	
Nǐ	_____	Yīngwén.	*(yeeng-wuhn)* English
Tā	_____	Fǎwén.	*(fah-wuhn)* French
Wǒmen	_____	Déwén.	*(duh-wuhn)* German
Nǐmen	_____	Rìwén.	*(ree-wuhn)* Japanese
Tāmen	_____	Zhōngwén.	

(my)
mài
to sell

Wǒ	_____	yú.	*(yoo)* fish
Nǐ	_____	xìpiào.	*(ssee-pee-ow)* theater tickets
Tā	_mài/_____	huār.	
Wǒmen	_____	zìxíngchē.	*(zih-sseeng-chuh)* bicycle
Nǐmen	_____	jiāojuǎn.	*(jee-ow-joo-ahn)* film
Tāmen	_____	shuǐ.	*(shway)* water

(zi) *(shwoh)* *(yee-bee-ahn)*
zài shuō yíbiàn *Shénme? Shénme?*
to repeat / say once again

Wǒ	_____	zhè ge cí.	*(juh)* this (M)
Nǐ	_____	nà ge cí.	*(nah)* that (M)
Tā	_____	míngzì.	*(meeng-zih)* name
Wǒmen	_____	nà ge wèntí.	*(wuhn-tee)* question
Nǐmen	_____	zhè ge wèntí.	
Tāmen	_____	zhèxiē xīn dòngcí.	*(juh-ssee-eh) (sseen) (dwong-tsih)* these new verbs

❏	**rénlèi** *(ruhn-lay)*	. . . .	mankind	人	_____
❏	**rénlì** *(ruhn-lee)*	. . . .	manpower		_____
❏	**rénqún** *(ruhn-choon)*	. . . .	crowd		_____
❏	**rénzào** *(ruhn-zow)*	. . . .	man-made		_____
❏	**rénzhǒng** *(ruhn-jwong)*	. . . .	human race	*rén*	_____

(shahng-bee-ahn)   *(ssee-ah-bee-ahn)*

Shàngbiān - Xiàbiān
above / over   below / under

Xiànzài wǒmen duō xuéxí jǐ ge cí. Zài Zhōngguó, zhèr yǒu yí ge fángzi. Qù your
(dwoh) *(ssee-yoo-eh-ssee)* *(jee)*   *(juhr)* *(yoh)* *(fahng-zuh)* *(choo)*
  more learn   several   here there is   house go to

(shway-fahng)   *(fahng-jee-ahn)*   *(dwong-ssee)*
shuǐfáng and look around the fángjiān. Let's xuéxí the míngzì of the dōngxi in the shuǐfáng,
bedroom   room   learn   names   things

just like wǒmen learned the various parts of the fángzi.
(fahng-zih)

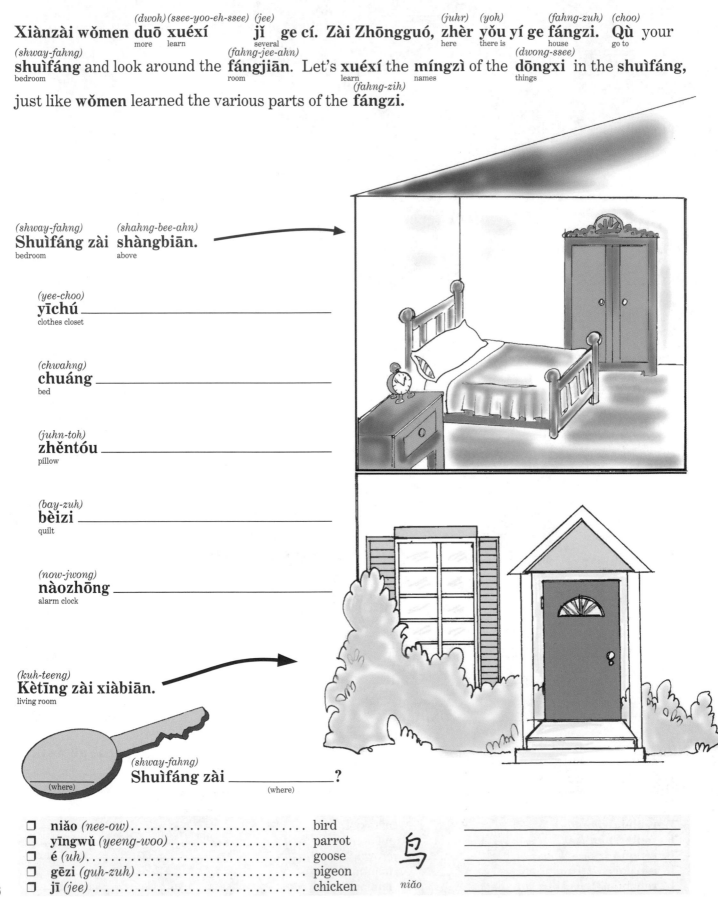

(shway-fahng)   *(shahng-bee-ahn)*
Shuǐfáng zài shàngbiān.
bedroom   above

(yee-choo)
yīchú _____
clothes closet

(chwahng)
chuáng _____
bed

(juhn-toh)
zhěntóu _____
pillow

(bay-zuh)
bèizi _____
quilt

(now-jwong)
nàozhōng _____
alarm clock

(kuh-teeng)
Kètīng zài xiàbiān.
living room

(shway-fahng)
Shuǐfáng zài _____?
(where)   (where)

(where)

☐	**niǎo** *(nee-ow)*............................	bird		_____
☐	**yīngwǔ** *(yeeng-woo)*.................	parrot	鸟	_____
☐	**é** *(uh)*....................................	goose		_____
☐	**gēzi** *(guh-zuh)*........................	pigeon		_____
☐	**jī** *(jee)*..................................	chicken	*niǎo*	_____

Xiànzài, remove the next group of stickers and label these **dōngxi** in your **shuìfáng** *(shway-fahng)*. Let's

move into the **yùshì** *(yoo-shr)* and do the same thing. Remember, **yùshì** *(yoo-shr)* means a room to bathe in. If

nǐ are in a **fànguǎn** *(fahn-gwahn)* and want the lavatory, **nǐ** want to ask for **cèsuǒ** *(tsuh-swoh)*, *not* for the **yùshì** *(yoo-shr)*. In

Zhōngguó, restrooms are marked with the Chinese characters 女 and 男 .

Don't confuse them! These would be two good characters to learn!

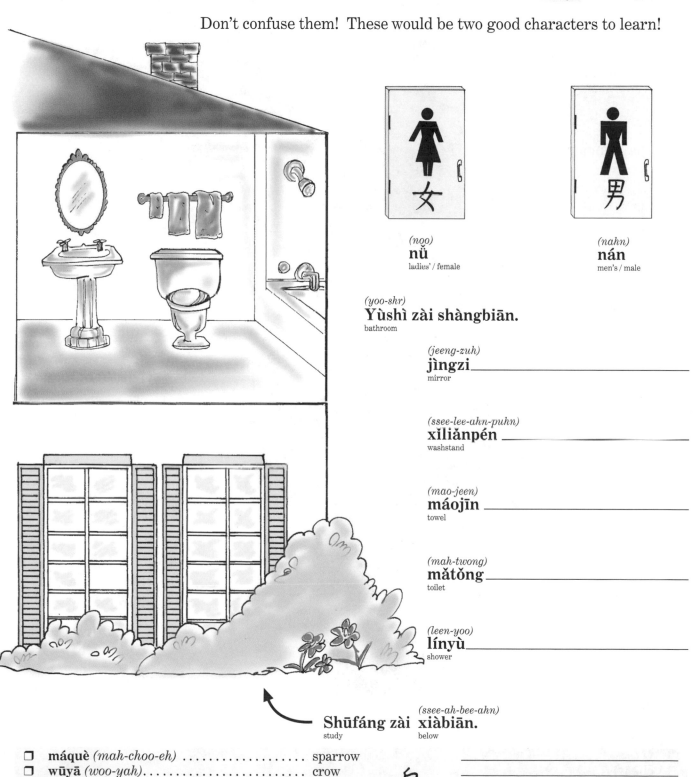

(noo)
nǚ
ladies' / female

(nahn)
nán
men's / male

(yoo-shr)
Yùshì zài shàngbiān.
bathroom

(jeeng-zuh)
jìngzi _____
mirror

(ssee-lee-ahn-puhn)
xǐliǎnpén _____
washstand

(mao-jeen)
máojīn _____
towel

(mah-twong)
mǎtǒng _____
toilet

(leen-yoo)
línyù _____
shower

Shūfáng zài xiàbiān.
study   *(ssee-ah-bee-ahn)* below

☐ **máquè** *(mah-choo-eh)* . . . . sparrow

☐ **wūyā** *(woo-yah)* . . . . crow

☐ **yā** *(yah)* . . . . duck

☐ **yīng** *(yeeng)* . . . . eagle

☐ **niǎolóng** *(nee-ow-lwong)* . . . . birdcage

鸟
niǎo

_____
_____
_____
_____
_____

Do not forget to remove the next group of stickers and label these *(dwong-ssee)* **dōngxi** in your *(fahng-zih)* **fángzi.** Okay,
things

it is time to review. Here's a quick quiz to see what you remember.

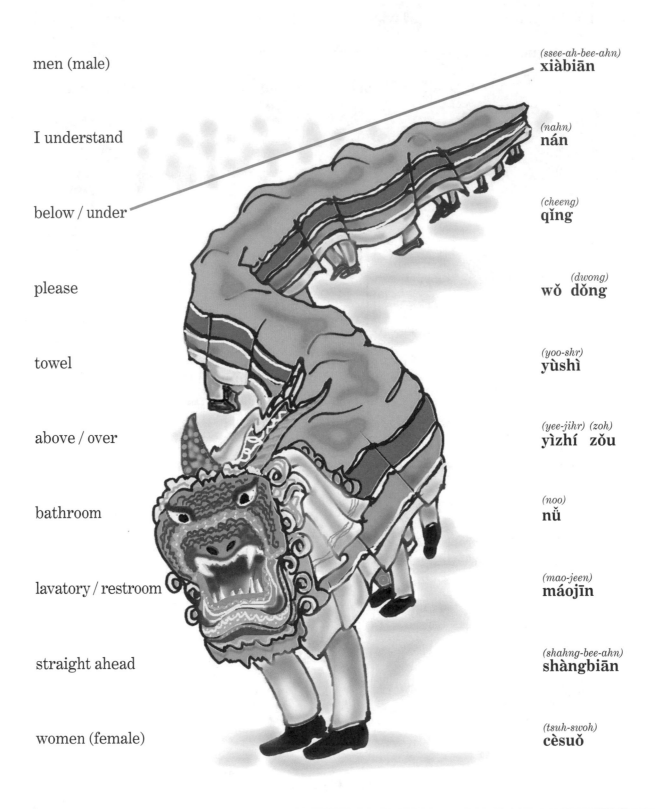

men (male)   *(ssee-ah-bee-ahn)* **xiàbiān**

I understand   *(nahn)* **nán**

below / under   *(cheeng)* **qǐng**

please   *(dwong)* **wǒ dǒng**

towel   *(yoo-shr)* **yùshì**

above / over   *(yee-jihr) (zoh)* **yìzhí zǒu**

bathroom   *(noo)* **nǔ**

lavatory / restroom   *(mao-jeen)* **máojīn**

straight ahead   *(shahng-bee-ahn)* **shàngbiān**

women (female)   *(tsuh-swoh)* **cèsuǒ**

❏ **yī** *(yee)* . . . . clothes
❏ **chènyī** *(chuhn-yee)*. shirt, blouse
❏ **dàyī** *(dah-yee)* . . . . overcoat
❏ **máoyī** *(mao-yee)* . . . . sweater
❏ **liányīqún** *(lee-ahn-yee-choon)* . . . . dress

衣
yī

Next stop — **shūfáng,** *(shoo-fahng)* specifically **zhuōzi** *(jwoh-zuh)* or **shūzhuō** *(shoo-jwoh)* in the **shūfáng!** **Shénme** *(shun-muh)* is on the
office table desk what

(jwoh-zuh)
zhuōzi? Let's identify the **dōngxi** *(dwong-ssee)* which one normally finds in the **shūfáng** or strewn about the
things

(fahng-zuh)
fángzi.
house

(dee-ahn-shr)
diànshì
television

_____

(chee-ahn-bee)
qiānbǐ
pencil

(gahng-bee)
gāngbǐ
pen

_____

_____

(dee-ahn-now)
diànnǎo
computer

(jihr)
zhǐ
paper

_____

_____

(zih-jihr-loh)
zìzhǐlǒu
wastebasket

(bao-jihr)
bàozhǐ
newspaper

(zah-jihr)
zázhì
magazine

bàozhǐ

(shoo)
shū
book

(yahn-jeeng)
yǎnjìng
eyeglasses

_____

_____

_____

❑ **shàngyī** *(shahng-yee)*	upper, outer garment	_____
❑ **nèiyī** *(nay-yee)*	undershirt	_____
❑ **shuìyī** *(shway-yee)*	pajamas	_____
❑ **yóuyǒngyī** *(yoh-yohng-yee)*	swimsuit	_____
❑ **yǔyī** *(yoo-yee)*	raincoat	_____

衣
yī

59

Don't forget these essentials!

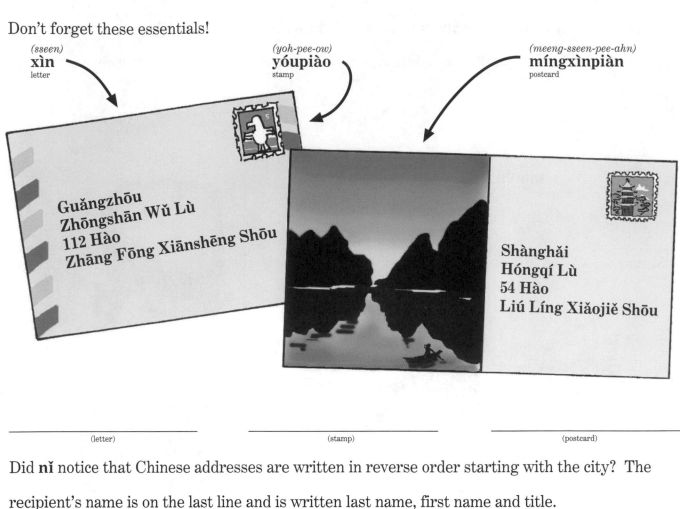

(sseen)
xìn
letter

(yoh-pee-ow)
yóupiào
stamp

(meeng-sseen-pee-ahn)
míngxìnpiàn
postcard

Guǎngzhōu
Zhōngshān Wǔ Lù
112 Hào
Zhāng Fōng Xiānshēng Shōu

Shànghǎi
Hóngqí Lù
54 Hào
Liú Líng Xiǎojiě Shōu

_____ (letter) _____ (stamp) _____ (postcard)

Did **nǐ** notice that Chinese addresses are written in reverse order starting with the city? The

recipient's name is on the last line and is written last name, first name and title.

(ssee-ahn-shuhng)
xiānshēng _____
Mr.

(tie-tie)
tàitài _____
Mrs.

(ssee-ow-jee-eh)
xiǎojiě _____
Miss

The word *(shoh)* **"shōu"** indicates the recipient and is used with both men and women. **Xiànzài** practice

saying and writing your name. **Nǐ jiào shénme míngzì? Wǒ jiào** _____.

Unless **nǐ** are very close friends, it is customary **zài Zhōngguó** to address an individual using the

appropriate title and his or her last name.

Remember these key **cí.**

(loo)
lù _____
road

(how)
hào _____
number

(jee-eh)
jiē _____
street

☐ **xié** *(ssee-eh)* . . . . shoes   _____
☐ **bùxié** *(boo-ssee-eh)* . . . . cotton shoes   鞋   _____
☐ **liángxié** *(lee-ahng-ssee-eh)* . . . . sandals   _____
☐ **qiúxié** *(chee-yoo-ssee-eh)* . . . . sport shoes   _____
☐ **tuōxié** *(twoh-ssee-eh)* . . . . slippers   *xié*   _____

Simple, isn't it? **Xiànzài**, after **nǐ** fill in the blanks below, go back a second time and negate

all these sentences by adding **"bù"** before each verb. Don't get discouraged! Just look at how

much **nǐ** have already learned and think ahead to wonderful new food, the Great Wall of China

and new adventures.

(kahn-jee-ahn)
kànjiàn _____
to see

(shway)
shuì _____
to sleep

(jee)
jì _____
to send by mail, mail

(jow)
zhǎo _____
to look for

(kahn-jee-ahn)
kànjiàn
to see

Wǒ _kànjiàn/_ _____ *(chwahng)* **chuáng.**

Nǐ _____ *(bay-zuh)* **bèizi.**
quilt

Tā _____ *(now-jwong)* **nàozhōng.**
alarm clock

Wǒmen _____ *(ssee-lee-ahn-puhn)* **xǐliǎnpén.**

Tāmen _____ *(leen-yoo)* **línyù.**
shower

(jee)
jì
to mail / send by mail

Wǒ _____ *(sseen)* **xìn.**
letters

Nǐ _____ *(moeng-sseen-pee-ahn)* **míngxìnpiàn.**
postcards

Tā _____ **shū.**

Wǒmen _____ **míngxìnpiàn.**

Nǐmen _____ **xìn.**

(shway)
shuì
to sleep

(zi) *(shway-fahng)*
Wǒ **zài shuìfáng** _____ .
in   bedroom

(fahng-zuh)
Nǐ **zài fángzi lǐ** _____ .
inside

(kuh-teeng)
Tā **zài kètīng** _____ .
living room

Wǒmen **zài shūfáng** _____ .

(nee-muhn) *(choo-fahng)*
Nǐmen **zài chúfáng** _____ .
kitchen

(dee-see-ah-shr)
Tāmen **zài dìxiàshì** _____ .
basement

(jow)
zhǎo
to look for

Wǒ _____ *(yoh-pee-ow)* **yóupiào.**

Nǐ _____ *(jihr)* **zhǐ.**

Tā _____ *(bao-jihr)* **bàozhǐ.**

(woh-muhn)
Wǒmen _____ *(gahng-bee)* **gāngbǐ.**

Nǐmen _zhǎo/_ _____ *(zah-jihr)* **zázhì.**

Tāmen _____ *(hwahr)* **huàr.**

☐ **qín** *(cheen)* . . . . musical instrument _____
☐ **fēngqín** *(fung-cheen)* . . . . organ _____
☐ **kǒuqín** *(koh-cheen)* . . . . harmonica _____
☐ **gāngqín** *(gahng-cheen)* . . . . piano _____
☐ **tíqín** *(tee-cheen)* . . . . violin _____

琴
qín

Before **nǐ** proceed with the next step, *(cheeng)* **qǐng,** identify all the items below.

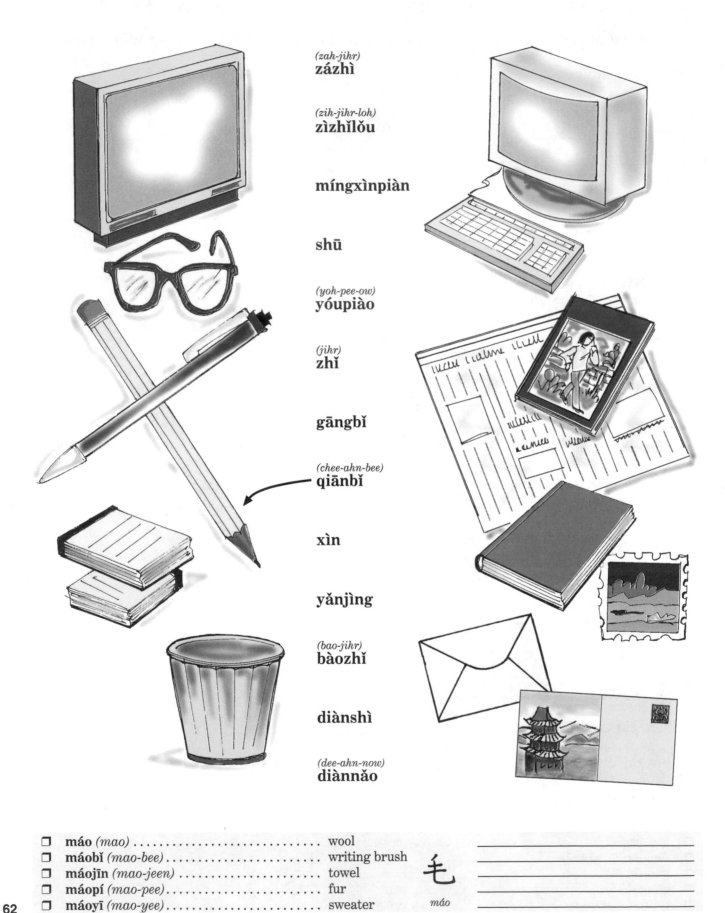

(zah-jihr)
zázhì

(zih-jihr-loh)
zìzhǐlǒu

míngxìnpiàn

shū

(yoh-pee-ow)
yóupiào

(jihr)
zhǐ

gāngbǐ

(chee-ahn-bee)
qiānbǐ

xìn

yǎnjìng

(bao-jihr)
bàozhǐ

diànshì

(dee-ahn-now)
diànnǎo

❏ **máo** *(mao)* . . . . wool
❏ **máobǐ** *(mao-bee)*. . . . . writing brush
❏ **máojīn** *(mao-jeen)* . . . . towel
❏ **máopí** *(mao-pee)*. . . . . fur
❏ **máoyī** *(mao-yee)* . . . . sweater

毛
máo

Xiànzài nǐ know how to count, how to ask **wèntí**, how to use **dòngcí** *(dwong-tsih)* with the "plug-in" formula,

how to make statements and how to describe something, be it the location of **yí ge lǚguǎn** *(loo-gwahn)* hotel

(hwoh-juh) *(fahng-zuh-duh)* *(yahn-suh)*
huòzhě yí ge fángzide yánsè. Xiànzài let's take the basics that **nǐ** have learned and expand
or house's color

them in special areas that will be most helpful in your travels. What does everyone do on a

(meeng-sseen-pee-ahn) *(yoh-joo)*
holiday? Send **míngxìnpiàn,** of course. Let's learn exactly how **Zhōngguó yóujú** works.
postcards post office

(sseen)
xìn . . .

(dow) *(may-gwoh)*
dào Měiguó
to

(ssee-bahn-yah)
dào Xībānyá
Spain

dào Yīngguó

(yee-dah-lee)
dào Yìdàlì
Italy

(yoh-joo) *(jee)* *(sseen)* *(meeng-sseen-pee-ahn)*
Zài Zhōngguó, yóujú has everything. **Nǐ jì xìn** and **míngxìnpiàn. Nǐ** also **mǎi**
send

(yoh-pee-ow) *(yoh-joo)* *(yoh-twong)* *(shr)* *(loo-suh)* *(ssee-oo-yow)*
yóupiào in the **yóujú. Zhōngguóde yóutǒng shì lǜsè de.** If **nǐ xūyào** to call home
stamps mailbox green need

(dow) *(yoh-joo)*
dào Měiguó or **Yīngguó,** sometimes this can also be done at **yóujú** as well as from a private
to

home or from your hotel.

❏ **dòu** *(doh)*	. . . .	bean	
❏ **dòufu** *(doh-foo)*	. . . .	bean curd	
❏ **dòushā** *(doh-shah)*	. . . .	bean paste	豆
❏ **dòuyá** *(doh-yah)*	. . . .	bean sprouts	
❏ **dòuyóu** *(doh-yoh)*	. . . .	soybean oil	*dòu*

Zhèr shì the necessary **yóuzhèng cí.** *(yoh-jung)* Practice them aloud and write them in the blanks.
postal

(sseen)
xìn
letter

(meeng-sseen-pee-ahn)
míngxìnpiàn
postcard

_____

_____

(bao-gwoh)
bāoguǒ
parcel

(dee-ahn-zih) (yoh-jee-ahn)
diànzi   yóujiàn
email

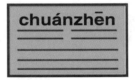
diànzi yóujiàn

_____

_____

(hahng-kwong-sseen)
hángkōngxìn
by airmail

航　空

(chwahn-juhn)
chuánzhēn
fax

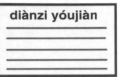
chuánzhēn

_____

_____

(yoh-pee-ow)
yóupiào
stamp

(dee-ahn-hwah) (teeng)
diànhuà   tíng
telephone   booth

_____

_____

(yoh-twong)
yóutǒng
mailbox

(dee-ahn-hwah)
diànhuà
telephone

_____

_____

❏ **mì** *(mee)*	honey	
❏ **mìfēng** *(mee-fung)*	honeybee	
❏ **mìjiàn** *(mee-jee-ahn)*	candied fruit	
❏ **mìyuè** *(mee-yoo-eh)*	honeymoon	
❏ **mìjú** *(mee-joo)*	tangerine	

蜜
mì

_____

_____

_____

_____

Next step — **nǐ** ask **wèntí** like those **xiàbiānde** *(ssee-ah-bee-ahn-duh)* depending on what **nǐ** would like. Repeat these sentences aloud many times.
below

(woh) *(zì)* *(nahr)* *(my)* *(yoh-pee-ow)*
Wǒ zài nǎr mǎi yóupiào? _____
I   where buy stamps

(meeng-sseen-pee-ahn)
Wǒ zài nǎr mǎi míngxìnpiàn? _____
postcards

(yoh) *(yoh-twong)*
Nǎr yǒu yóutǒng? _____
is   mailbox

(gohng-yohng) *(dee-ahn-hwah)*
Nǎr yǒu gōngyòng diànhuà? _____
public   telephone

(dah) *(dee-ahn-hwah)*
Wǒ zài nǎr dǎ diànhuà? _____
make telephone calls

(dah) *(buhn-dee)* *(dee-ahn-hwah)*
Wǒ zài nǎr dǎ běndì diànhuà? _____
make local   telephone call

(dah) *(chahng-too)* *(dee-ahn-hwah)*
Wǒ zài nǎr dǎ chángtú diànhuà? _____
make long-distance

(dwoh-shao) *(chee-ahn)*
Duōshao qián? _____ *Duōshao qián? Duōshao qián? Duōshao qián?*

Xiànzài, quiz yourself. See if **nǐ** can translate the following thoughts into **Zhōngwén.**

1.   Where is a telephone booth? _____

2.   Where do I make a telephone call? _____

3.   Where do I make a local telephone call? _____

4.   Where is the post office? _____

5.   Where do I buy stamps? _____

6.   How much is it? _____

7.   Where do I send a package? _____

8.   Where do I send a fax? _____

(shr) *(jee)*
Zhèr shì jǐ ge dòngcí.
are   several

(dah)
dǎ _____
to make (telephone call)

(gay)
gěi _____
to give

(ssee-eh)
xiě _____
to write

(foo) *(chee-ahn)*
fù qián _____
to pay, pay the price

Practice these verbs by not only filling in the blanks, but by saying them aloud many, many

times until **nǐ** are comfortable with the sounds and the **cí.**

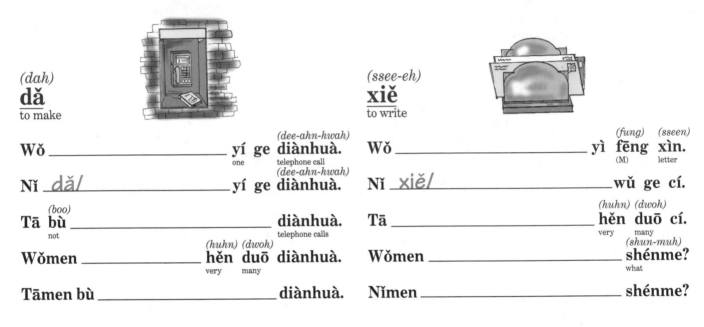

(dah)
dǎ
to make

Wǒ _____ **yí ge diànhuà.**
                          one *(dee-ahn-hwah)* telephone call

Nǐ _dǎ/_____ **yí ge diànhuà.**
                          (dee-ahn-hwah)

Tā bù _____ **diànhuà.**
      not   telephone calls

Wǒmen _____ **hěn duō diànhuà.**
               (huhn) *(dwoh)*
               very many

Tāmen bù _____ **diànhuà.**

(ssee-eh)
xiě
to write

Wǒ _____ **yì fēng xìn.**
                          (fung) *(sseen)*
                          (M)   letter

Nǐ _xiě/_____ **wǔ ge cí.**

Tā _____ **hěn duō cí.**
                          (huhn) *(dwoh)*
                          very many

Wǒmen _____ **shénme?**
                        (shun-muh)
                        what

Nǐmen _____ **shénme?**

(gay)
gěi
to give

Wǒ _____ **tā yì běn shū.**
                          (tah) *(buhn)*
                          him (M)

Nǐ _gěi/_____ **wǒ sì zhāng míngxìnpiàn.**
                   (sih) *(jahng)*
                   me   (M)

Tā _____ **tāmen hěn duō qián.**
                  them very much money
                  (huhn) *(dwoh)*

Wǒmen _____ **tā bā zhāng yóupiào.**
                   her eight (M) stamps
                   (jahng) *(yoh-pee-ow)*

Tāmen _____ **nǐ shénme?**
                       you what
                       (shun-muh)

(foo) *(chee-ahn)*
fù qián
to pay (the price)

Wǒ _____ **yì běn shūde** _____ .
                (buhn) *(shoo-duh)*
                (M) book's

Nǐ _fù/_____ **qiānbǐde** _qián/_ .
                 (chee-ahn-bee-duh)
                 pencil's

Tā _____ **gāngbǐde** _____ .
                  (gahng-bee-duh)
                  fountain pen's

Wǒmen _____ **wǔ zhāng yóupiàode** _____ .
                 (yoh-pee-ow-duh)
                 stamp's

Tāmen bù ___ **shénme** _____ ?
                  what

☐ **niú** *(nee-oo)*	cow
☐ **niúdú** *(nee-oo-doo)*	calf
☐ **niújiǎo** *(nee-oo-jee-ow)*	horn
☐ **niúzǎikù** *(nee-oo-zi-koo)*	jeans
☐ **niúnǎi** *(nee-oo-ni)*	milk

牛

niú _____
_____
_____
_____
_____

Zhèr shì some of the most important **Zhōngguó** signs. Spend some time becoming familiar with

(tah-muhn)
tāmen. Take a piece of paper and try drawing them yourself.
them

(loo)   *(ahn)*
Yí lù píng ān!
safe and peaceful journey

Hot

Cold

Push

Pull

Vacant

For Hire, For Rent

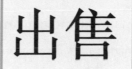
For Sale

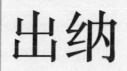
Cashier

Ticket Office

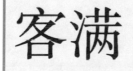
Sold Out

Closed

No Photos Allowed

Danger

Stop

Do Not Touch

Yí lù píng ān!

What follows are approximate conversions, so when you order something by liters, kilograms or grams you will have an idea of what to expect and not find yourself being handed one piece of candy when you thought you ordered an entire bag.

To Convert		Do the Math		
liters (l) to gallons,	multiply by 0.26	4 liters x 0.26	=	1.04 gallons
gallons to liters,	multiply by 3.79	10 gal. x 3.79	=	37.9 liters
kilograms (kg) to pounds,	multiply by 2.2	2 kilograms x 2.2	=	4.4 pounds
pounds to kilos,	multiply by 0.46	10 pounds x 0.46	=	4.6 kg
grams (g) to ounces,	multiply by 0.035	100 grams x 0.035	=	3.5 oz.
ounces to grams,	multiply by 28.35	10 oz. x 28.35	=	283.5 g.
meters (m) to feet,	multiply by 3.28	2 meters x 3.28	=	6.56 feet
feet to meters,	multiply by 0.3	6 feet x 0.3	=	1.8 meters

For fun, take your weight in pounds and convert it into kilograms. It sounds better that way, doesn't it? How many kilometers is it from your home to school, to work, to the post office?

The Simple Versions		
one liter	=	approximately one US quart
four liters	=	approximately one US gallon
one kilo	=	approximately 2.2 pounds
100 grams	=	approximately 3.5 ounces
500 grams	=	slightly more than one pound
one meter	=	slightly more than three feet

The distance between London and **Běijīng** is approximately 5,063 miles. How many kilometers would that be? It is 9,525 miles between New York and Singapore. How many kilometers is that?

kilometers (km.) to miles,	multiply by 0.62	1000 km. x 0.62	=	620 miles
miles to kilometers,	multiply by 1.6	1000 miles x 1.6	=	1,600 km.

Inches	1		2		3		4		5		6		7

To convert centimeters into inches, multiply by 0.39   Example: 9 cm. x 0.39 = 3.51 in.

To convert inches into centimeters, multiply by 2.54   Example: 4 in. x 2.54 = 10.16 cm.

cm 1	2	3	4	5	6	7	8	9	10	11	12	13	14	15	16	17	18

(fah) *(pee-ow)*
Fā Piào
(the) bill

Zài Zhōngguó, there are also bills to pay. **Nǐ** have just finished your meal and **nǐ** would like to

pay the bill. **Nǐ zěnme fù qián? Nǐ jiào** the **fúwùyuán.** The **fúwùyuán** will normally reel
(zuhn-muh) *(foo)* *(chee-ahn)* *(jee-ow)* *(foo-woo-yoo-ahn)*
how pay call service person

off what **nǐ** have eaten while writing rapidly. **Tā** will then **gěi** you a slip of **zhǐ,** and say,
(gay) *(jihr)*
give paper

(yee-gohng) *(woo-shr-lee-oo)* *(kwhy)* *(mao)*
" Yígòng wǔshíliù kuài liù máo."
altogether

Nǐ will take your **fā piào** to the counter to pay the cashier **huòzhě nǐ gěi fúwùyuán qián**
(fah)(pee-ow) *(hwoh-juh)* *(gay)* *(chee-ahn)*
bill or give money

and **fā piào.**
(fah)(pee-ow)

Remember that, **zài Zhōngguó,** it is not customary to leave a tip. Also do not be surprised if the
(foo-woo-yoo-ahn)
fúwùyuán does not thank you – this is also not a custom **zài Zhōngguó.** Sound confusing? Not
(fah)(pee-ow)
(sseen)
really, just **xīn** and different. Every night after dinner practice asking for the **fā piào** in

Zhōngwén.

Note: **Lǚguǎn** is a general term for hotels. Many foreign tourists visiting China stay in a
(loo-gwahn)
(been-gwahn) *(jee-oo-dee-ahn)*
bīnguǎn or **jiǔdiàn** which are more comfortably appointed.

☐ **niúpái** *(nee-oo-pie)* . . . . beefsteak
☐ **niúpí** *(nee-oo-pee)* . . . . leather
☐ **niúpí zhǐ** *(nee-oo-pee)(jihr)* . . . . brown paper
☐ **niúròu** *(nee-oo-roh)* . . . . beef
☐ **niúwěi** *(nee-oo-way)* . . . . oxtail

牛

niú

Remember these key **cí** when dining out **zài Zhōngguó.**

(foo-woo-yoo-ahn)
fúwùyuán _____
waiter

(shoh-joo)
shōujù _____
receipt

(fah)(pee-ow)
fā piào   *fā piào* _____
bill

(cheeng-wuhn)
qǐngwèn _____
excuse me, may I ask . . .

(tsi-dahn)
càidān _____
menu

(boo) (ssee-eh)
bú xiè _____
you're welcome

(dway-boo-chee)
duìbùqǐ _____
excuse me

(ssee-eh-ssee-eh) or *(shee-shee)*
xièxie _____
thank you

(cheeng)
qǐng _____
please

(gay) (woh)
gěi wǒ _____
give me

(juhr) *(shr)*
Zhèr shì yí ge sample **duìhuà** involving paying the **fā piào** when leaving a **lǚguǎn.**
this   is   (M)   *(dway-hwah)* conversation   *(fah)(pee-ow)* bill   *(loo-gwahn)*

Zhāng Sān:	**Xiānshēng, wǒ xiǎng jié zhàng.** *(jee-eh)* want to clear _Xiānshēng, wǒ xiǎng jié zhàng. Xiānshēng, wǒ xiǎng jié zhàng._
Lǚguǎn Jīnglǐ: *(loo-gwahn) (jeeng-lee)* manager	**Qǐngwèn nǎ ge fángjiān?** *(cheeng-wuhn)* *(fahng-jee-ahn)* excuse me, may I ask which room _____
Zhāng Sān:	**Sān bǎi yì shí hào.** *(by)* *(how)* hundred number _____
Lǚguǎn Jīnglǐ:	**Xièxie. Qǐng děng yí xià.** *(ssee-eh-ssee-eh) (cheeng) (dung) (ssee-ah)* please wait a little _____
Lǚguǎn Jīnglǐ:	**Zhèr shì nǐde fā piào.** *(juhr) (shr) (nee-duh) (fah)(pee-ow)* your bill _____

If **nǐ yǒu** *(yoh)* any problems with **shùzì,** *(shoo-zuh)* just ask someone to write out the **shùzì,** so that **nǐ** can be
have

sure you understand everything correctly,

"Qǐng xiě chū shùzì géi wǒ kàn. Xièxie." *(ssee-eh) (choo)* *(gay)* *(ssee-eh-ssee-eh)*
please   write   out   for   me   to see

Practice: _____
(Please write out the number for me to see. Thank you.)

- ❏ **yǐ** *(yee)* .... chair _____
- ❏ **chángyǐ** *(chahng-yee)* .... bench _____
- ❏ **tǎngyǐ** *(tahng-yee)* .... recliner 椅 _____
- ❏ **yáoyǐ** *(yow-yee)* .... rocking chair _____
- ❏ **zhuànyǐ** *(jwahn-yee)* .... swivel chair   *yǐ* _____

Xiànzài, let's take a break from **fā piào hé qián** *(fah)(pee-ow)(huh)(chee-ahn)* and learn some fun **xīn cí. Nǐ** can always *(sseen)*

practice these **cí** by using your flash cards at the back of this book. Carry these flash cards in

your purse, pocket, briefcase **huòzhě** knapsack and *use them!*

(ki)
kāi
open
_____

(gwahn)
guān
closed
_____

(dah)
dà
big
_____

(ssee-ow)
xiǎo
small

(jee-ahn-kahng)
jiànkāng
healthy
_____

(beeng)
bìng
sick

(how)
hǎo
good
_____

(hwhy) (boo)(how)
huài / bù hǎo
bad
_____

(ruh)
rè
hot
_____

(lung)
lěng
cold
_____

☐ **guǎn** (*gwahn*) . . . . place, hall
☐ **bówùguǎn** (*bwoh-woo-gwahn*) . . . . museum
☐ **cháguǎn** (*chah-gwahn*) . . . . teahouse
☐ **lǚguǎn** (*loo-gwahn*) . . . . hotel
☐ **lǐfàguǎn** (*lee-fah-gwahn*) . . . . barber shop

馆
guǎn
_____
_____
_____
_____

(dwahn)
duǎn _____
short

(chahng)
cháng _____
long

(mahn)
màn _____
slow

(kwhy)
kuài _____
fast

(gao)
gāo _____
tall

(I)
ǎi _____
short

(lao)
lǎo _____
old

(nee-ahn-cheeng)
niánqīng _____
young

(gway)
guì _____
expensive

(pee-ahn-yee)
piányí _____
inexpensive

(yoh-chee-en)
yǒuqián _____
rich

(chee-oong)
qióng _____
poor

(dwoh)
duō _____
a lot

(shao)
shǎo _____
a little

❏ **měishùguǎn** _(may-shoo-gwahn)_ . . . . art gallery
❏ **shuǐzúguǎn** _(shway-zoo-gwahn)_ . . . . aquarium
❏ **tǐyùguǎn** _(tee-yoo-gwahn)_ . . . . gymnasium
❏ **túshūguǎn** _(too-shoo-gwahn)_ . . . . library
❏ **zhǎnlǎnguǎn** _(jahn-lahn-gwahn)_ . . . . exhibition hall

馆
guǎn _____
_____
_____
_____

(juhr) *(shr)* *(sih)* *(sseen)* *(dwong-tsih)*
Zhèr shì sì ge xīn dòngcí.
four   new

(jihr-dow)
zhīdào _____
to know

(nung)
néng _____
to be able to, can

(kahn)
kàn _____
to read, look at

(yeeng-gi)
yīnggāi _____
to have to, should

Study the patterns below closely, as **nǐ** will use these **dòngcí** a lot.
verbs

(jihr-dow)
zhīdào
to know

Chángchéng Fàndiàn

Wǒ _____ **nà ge.**
that

Nǐ _____ **yìdiǎn Zhōngwén.**
(yee-dee-ahn)
a little

Tā _____ **hěn duō.**
(huhn) (dwoh)
very   much

Wǒmen bù _____ **hěn duō.**

Tāmen bù _____ .

(nung)
néng
to be able to / can

Wǒ _____ **kàn Zhōngwén.**
read

Nǐ _____ **shuō Zhōngwén.**
(shwoh)
speak

Tā *néng/* _____ **dǒng Zhōngwén.**
(dwong)
understand

Wǒmen _____ **dǒng Yīnggwén.**

Nǐmen _____ **kàn Zhōngwén.**

(kahn)
kàn
to read / look at

Wǒ _____ **shū.**

Nǐ _____ **zázhì.**
(zah-jihr)
magazine

Tā _____ **míngxìnpiàn.**
(meeng-sseen-pee-ahn)
postcard

Wǒmen _____ **biǎogé.**
(bee-ow-guh)
form

Nǐmen _____ **hěn duō.**
(huhn) (dwoh)
very   much

(yeeng-gi)
yīnggāi
to have to / should

Wǒ _____ **shuō Zhōngwén.**

Nǐ _____ **kàn shū.**

Tā _____ **shuō Yīngwén.**

Wǒmen _____ **dǒng Zhōngwén.**
(dwong)
understand

Tāmen _____ **kàn bàozhǐ.**
(bao-jihr)
newspaper

❐ **mǐ** *(mee)* . . . . rice _____
❐ **mǐfàn** *(mee-fahn)* . . . . cooked rice _____
❐ **mǐfěn** *(mee-fuhn)* . . . . rice noodle _____
❐ **mǐjiǔ** *(mee-jee-oo)* . . . . rice wine _____
❐ **mǐsè** *(mee-suh)* . . . . cream-colored _____

米
mǐ

Notice that "**néng**," *(nung)* am able to **hé** "**yīnggāi**," *(yeeng-gi)* have to along with "**xiǎng**" *(ssee-ahng)* want can be combined with another verb.

Wǒ xiǎng xuéxí *(ssee-yoo-eh-ssee)* want to learn **Zhōngwén.**	

Wǒ xiǎng xuéxí Zhōngwén.
want   to learn

Wǒmen xiǎng xuéxí Zhōngwén.

Wǒ néng dǒng Zhōngwén.
(nung) *(dwong)* *(jwong-wuhn)*
can   understand

Wǒmen néng dǒng Zhōngwén.

Wǒ yīnggāi kàn shū.
(yeeng-gi)
have to   read

Wǒmen yīnggāi kàn shū.

Wǒ shuō Zhōngwén.
(shwoh) *(jwong-wuhn)*
speak

Wǒ néng shuō Zhōngwén.
(shwoh)
can

Wǒ yīnggāi shuō Zhōngwén.
have to

Wǒ xiǎng shuō Zhōngwén.
want

Nǐ néng *(nung)* can translate these thoughts into **Zhōngwén ma?** The answers **zài xiàbiān.** *(ssee-ah-bee-ahn)* below

1. I can speak French. _____

2. They have to pay now. _____

3. He wants to pay. _____

4. We don't know. _____

5. She knows very much. _____

6. I can speak a little Chinese. _____

7. I cannot understand English. _____

8. We are not able to (cannot) understand German. _____

9. I want to read the newspaper. _____

10. She reads the magazine. _____

Xiànzài, draw **xiàn** *(ssee-ahn)* lines between the opposites below. Do not forget to say them out loud. Use these **cí** every day to describe *(dwong-ssee)* **dōngxi** things **zài** *(nee-duh)* **nǐde** your **fángzi,** **nǐde** *(ssee-yoo-eh-ssee-ow)* **xuéxiào** school or **nǐde** your *(bahn-gohng-shr)* **bàngōngshì.** office

(gao) **gāo**

(ssee-ah) **xià**

(nee-ahn-cheeng) **niánqīng**

(chee-oong) **qióng**

(jee-ahn-kahng) **jiànkāng**

(chahng) **cháng**

(dwoh) **duō**

(how) **hǎo**

(ruh) **rè**

(zwoh) **zuǒ**

(mahn) **màn**

(gway) **guì**

(ssee-ow) **xiǎo**

(shahng) **shàng**

(I) **ǎi**

(shao) **shǎo**

(dah) **dà**

(pee-ahn-yee) **piányí**

(beeng) **bīng**

(lao) **lǎo**

(kwhy) **kuài**

(yoh) **yòu**

(lung) **lěng**

(yoh-chee-en) **yǒuqián**

(hwhy) **huài**

(dwahn) **duǎn**

❑	**yuè** *(yoo-eh)*	month, moon
❑	**yuèbào** *(yoo-eh-bao)*	monthly magazine
❑	**yuèliang** *(yoo-eh-lee-ahng)*	moon
❑	**yuèsè** *(yoo-eh-suh)*	moonlight
❑	**yuèyè** *(yoo-eh-yeh)*	moonlit night

月

yuè

75

(loo-kuh) *(loo-sseeng)*
Lǚkè Lǚxíng
traveler   travels

(zwoh-tee-ahn) (dow)
Zuótiān dào Nánjīng!
yesterday   to

(jeen-tee-ahn)
Jīntiān dào Shànghǎi!
today

(meeng-tee-ahn)
Míngtiān dào Běijīng!
tomorrow

(loo-sseeng) (huhn) (rohng-yee)   *(ruhn) (doh) (huhn)*   *(huh)*
Zài Zhōngguó, lǚxíng hěn róngyì. Zhōngguó rén dōu hěn helpful. **Zhōngguó hé**
            travel   very   easy   people all   very

(may-gwoh) (chah-boo-dwoh) (yee-yahng) (dah)   *(yoh) (huhn)*
Měiguó chàbùduō yíyàng dà. Zài Zhōngguó yǒu hěn many ways **lǚxíng:**
about   same   size   there are very   to travel

(chee) (zih-sseeng-chuh)
qí zìxíngchē
ride bicycle

(zwoh) (sahn-loon-chuh)
zuò sānlúnchē
by   pedicab

(chwahn)
zuò chuán
boat

(zwoh) (hwoh-chuh)
zuò huǒchē
by   train

(fay-jee)
zuò fēijī
airplane

(gohng-gohng-chee-chuh)
zuò gōnggòngqìchē

+11	+12 -12	-11	-10	-9	-8	-7	-6	-5	-4	-3	-2	-1	GMT

DATELINE

ASIA

NORTH AMERICA

SUNDAY SATURDAY

AFRICA

SOUTH AMERICA

When **nǐ** are traveling, **nǐ** will want to tell others your nationality and **nǐ** will meet people from all corners of the world. Can you guess where people are from if they say one of the following?

The answers are in your glossary beginning on page 108.

(woh) (tswong) (yeeng-gwoh)   (lie)
Wǒ cóng Yīngguó lái. _____

(tswong) (yeen-doo-nee-ssee-yah) (lie)
Wǒmen cóng Yìndùníxīyà   lái. _____

(yee-dah-lee)
Wǒ cóng Yìdàlì lái. _____

(duh-gwoh)
Wǒmen cóng Déguó lái. _____

(may-gwoh)
Wǒ cóng Měiguó lái. _____

(muhng-goo)
Wǒmen cóng Měnggǔ lái. _____

(ssee-bahn-yah)
Wǒ cóng Xībānyá lái. _____

(ree-buhn)
Wǒmen cóng Rìběn lái. _____

(ow-dah-lee-yah)
Wǒ cóng Àodàlìyà lái. _____

(sseen-ssee-lahn)
Tā cóng Xīnxīlán lái. _____

(lao-woh)
Wǒ cóng Lǎowō lái. _____

(yeen-doo)
Tā cóng Yìndù lái. _____

(huh-lahn)
Wǒ cóng Hélán lái. _____

(duhn-my)
Tā cóng Dānmài lái. _____

(yoo-eh-nahn)
Wǒ cóng Yuènán lái. _____

(tie-gwoh)
Tā cóng Tàiguó lái. _____

(nwoh-way)
Wǒ cóng Nuówēi lái. _____

(jee-ah-nah-dah)
Tā cóng Jiānádà   lái. _____

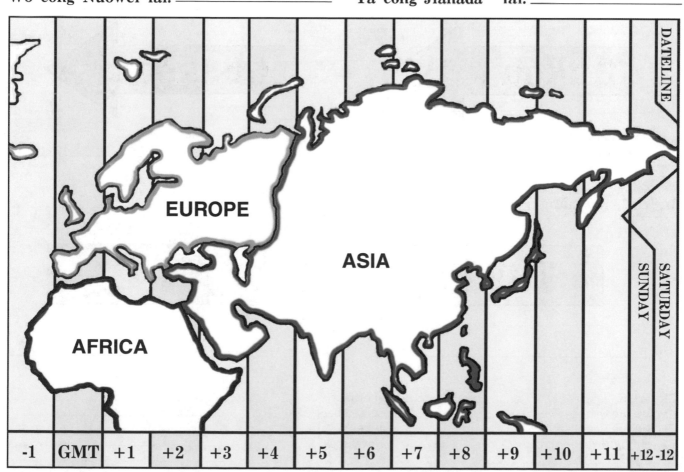

| -1 | GMT | +1 | +2 | +3 | +4 | +5 | +6 | +7 | +8 | +9 | +10 | +11 | +12 -12 |

Due to the amount of **wàiguó** *(why-gwoh)* visitors in **Zhōngguó,** you will see many "travel" **cí.** Practice
foreign

saying the following **cí** many times. **Nǐ** will see them often.

(ssee-ahng)
xiàng _____
lane

(loo-sseng) *(shuh)*
lǚxíng shè _____
travel agent

(loo-kuh)
lǚkè _____
passenger, traveler

(seeng-lee)
xínglǐ _____
luggage, baggage

(jee-eh)
jiē _____
street

(sseng-lee) *(chuh)*
xínglǐ chē _____
baggage cart

(dah-dow)
dàdào _____
boulevard

(ruhn-sseeng-dow)
rénxíngdào _____
sidewalk

Xiàbiān shì four **cí** which should help you whenever you travel in and out of the country.

(wuhn-jee-ahn)
wénjiàn
documents

(hoo-jow)
hùzhào
passport

(chee-ahn-jung)
qiānzhèng
visa

(jee-ahn-kahng) *(jung-meeng)* *(shoo)*
jiànkāng zhèngmíng shū
health certificate

Zhèr shì some basic signs which **nǐ yě** *(yuh)* should learn to recognize quickly.
also

(roo-koh)
rùkǒu _____
entrance

(choo-koh)
chūkǒu _____
exit

Rùkǒu 入口

Chūkǒu 出口

(jeen) *(jihr)* *(twong)* *(sseeng)*
jìn zhǐ tōng xíng _____
no trespassing

(tie-peeng) *(muhn)*
tàipíng mén _____
emergency gate

(jeen) *(jihr)* *(jow-ssee-ahng)*
jìn zhǐ zhàoxiàng _____
no photos allowed

(chee-eh) *(woo)* *(roo-nay)*
qiè wù rùnèi _____
keep out

Tuī 推

Lā 拉

(tway)
tuī _____
push (doors)

(lah)
lā _____
pull (doors)

❏ **èryuè** *(ur-yoo-eh)* . . . . February
❏ **jiǔyuè** *(jee-oo-yoo-eh)* . . . . September
❏ **liùyuè** *(lee-oo-yoo-eh)* . . . . June
❏ **shíyīyuè** *(shr-yee-yoo-eh)* . . . . November
❏ **sìyuè** *(sih-yoo-eh)* . . . . April

月 _____
_____
_____
_____
yuè

Let's learn the basic travel verbs. Take out a piece of paper and make up your own sentences with these **xīn cí.** Follow the same pattern **nǐ** have in previous Steps.

(fay)
fēi _____
to fly

(dow)
dào _____
to arrive

(ki)
kāi _____
to leave, depart

(deeng)
dìng _____
to book, reserve

(loo-sseeng)
lǚxíng _____
to travel

(hwahn) (chuh)
huàn chē _____
to transfer vehicles

(shoh-shr)
shōushi _____
to pack

(zwoh)
zuò _____
to sit, ride in

Zhèr are more *(sseen)* **xīn cí** for your trip.
new

(fay-jee-chahng)
fēijīchǎng
airport

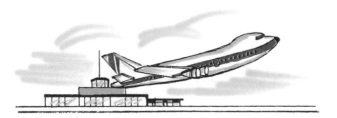

(hwoh-chuh) (yoo-eh-tie)
huǒchē yuètái
train   platform

(shr-jee-ahn) (bee-ow)
shíjiān biǎo
time   schedule

Cóng Shànghǎi dào Nánjīng		
Kāi	**Huǒchē**	**Dào**
08:30	Kuàichē	10:30
11:10	Kuàichē	13:10
13:25	Pǔtōngchē	19:25
16:15	Pǔtōngchē	22:15

(hwoh-chuh) (zwong) (jahn)
huǒchē zǒng zhàn
train   main   station

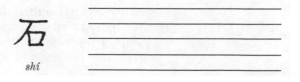

❏ **shí** *(shr)* . . . . stone, rock
❏ **shídiāo** *(shr-dee-ow)* . . . . carved stone
❏ **shíkuài** *(shr-kwhy)* . . . . boulder
❏ **shímò** *(shr-mwoh)* . . . . graphite
❏ **shíyīng** *(shr-yeeng)* . . . . quartz

石
shí

_____
_____
_____
_____
_____

With **zhè** *(juh)* **xiē** *(ssee-eh)* **dòngcí,** *(dwong-tsih)* **nǐ** are ready for any **lǚxíng** *(loo-sseeng)* anywhere. **Nǐ** should have no problems

these several

with these verbs, just remember the basic "plug-in" formula **nǐ** have already learned. Use that

knowledge to translate the following thoughts into **Zhōngwén.** The answers **zài xiàbiān.** *(ssee-ah-bee-ahn)*

1.   I fly to Nanjing. _____

2.   I pack tomorrow. _____

3.   We travel to Kunming. _____

4.   He sits in the airplane. _____

5.   She books the flight to go to America. _____

6.   They travel to Hangzhou. _____

7.   Where is the train to Xi'an? _____

8.   How can we fly to Japan? _____

Zhèr are some **zhòngyàode cí** *(jwong-yow-duh)* for the **lǚke.** *(loo-kuh)*

important   traveler

Cóng Shànghǎi dào Nánjīng		
Kāi	Huǒchē	Dào
08:30	Kuàichē	10:30
11:10	Kuàichē	13:10
13:25	Pǔtōngchē	19:25
16:15	Pǔtōngchē	22:15

(yoh-ruhn)
yǒurén _____
occupied

(dway-hwahn) (choo)
duìhuàn chù _____
money-exchange office

(chuh-ssee-ahng)
chēxiāng _____
compartment

(zwoh-way)
zuòwèi _____
seat

(dow)
dào _____
to arrive, arrival

(ki)
kāi _____
to depart, departure

(gwoh-why)
guówài _____
international

(gwoh-nay)
guónèi _____
domestic

Increase your travel **cí** by writing out the **xiàbiānde** *(ssee-ah-bee-ahn-duh)* **cí** and practicing the sample

sentences out loud. Substitute your destination and practice using different numbers.

(dow)
dào _____
to
　　　　　　　　　　　Dào Shànghǎi de huǒchē zài nǎr?

(shoh-pee-ow) *(choo)*
shòupiào chù _____
ticket　　　office
　　　　　　　　　　　Shòupiào chù zài nǎr?

(shr-woo) *(jow-leeng)*
shīwù zhāolǐng _____
lost-and-found office
　　　　　　　　　　　Shīwù zhāolǐng zài nǎr?

(sseeng-lee) *(chuh)*
xínglǐ chē ____ *Nǎr yǒu xínglǐ chē? Nǎr yǒu xínglǐ chē?*
baggage　cart
　　　　　　　　　　　Nǎr yǒu xínglǐ chē?

(tee-eh-gway)
tiěguǐ _____
track
　　　　　　　　　　　Dìqī tiáo tiěguǐ zài nǎr?
　　　　　　　　　　　seventh (M)

(yoo-eh-tie)
yuètái _____
platform
　　　　　　　　　　　Dìbā yuètái zài nǎr?
　　　　　　　　　　　eighth

(dway-hwahn) *(choo)*
duìhuàn chù _____
money-exchange　office
　　　　　　　　　　　Nǎr yǒu duìhuàn chù?

(gway-tie)
guìtái _____
counter
　　　　　　　　　　　Bā hào guìtái zài nǎr?

(hoh-chuh-shr)
hòuchēshì _____
waiting room
　　　　　　　　　　　Hòuchēshì zài nǎr?

(tsahn-chuh)
cānchē _____
dining car
　　　　　　　　　　　Zhè ge huǒchē yǒu cānchē ma?

(woh-poo)
wòpù _____
sleeping car
　　　　　　　　　　　Zhè ge huǒchē yǒu wòpù ma?

(tahng-yee)
tǎngyǐ _____
reclining car
　　　　　　　　　　　Zhè ge huǒchē yǒu tǎngyǐ ma?

_____ *(fay-jee)* *(ki)*
(when) **Fēijī** _____ **kāi?**
　　　　airplane (when)

_____ **Nà shì** _____ ?
(what)　　　　　　(what)

❑ **bǎoshí** *(bao-shr)* . . . . gem　_____
❑ **hǎi lán bǎoshí** *(hi)(lahn)(bao-shr)* . . . . aquamarine　_____
❑ **hóng bǎoshí** *(hohng)(bao-shr)* . . . . ruby　石 _____
❑ **lán bǎoshí** *(lahn)(bao-shr)* . . . . sapphire　_____
❑ **zuànshí** *(zwahn-shr)* . . . . diamond　*shí* _____

81

Xiàbiānde *(ssee-ah-bee-ahn-duh)* **nǐ** *(nung)* **néng** *(kahn)* **kàn ma?**
  can read

← **Xiànzài nǐ zuò zài fēi qù Zhōngguó** *(zwoh)* sit *(fay)* fly *(choo)*
de fēijī shàng. *(fay-jee)* airplane on **Nǐ yǒu le piào,** *(pee-ow)* ticket
qián hé hùzhào. *(chee-ahn)* money *(hoo-jow)* passport **Nǐ dài le nǐde** *(die)* bring your *(nee-duh)* *(loo-kuh)*
xiāngzi. *(ssee-ahng-zuh)* suitcase **Xiànzài nǐ shì yí ge lǚkè.** *(shr)* are *(loo-kuh)* traveler
Nǐ shísì xiǎoshí hòu zài Zhōngguó *(shr-sih)* fourteen *(ssee-ow-shr)* hours *(hoh)* after
jiàngluò. *(jee-ahng-lwoh)* land

Yí lù píng ān!
safe and peaceful journey

Zhōngguó huǒchē come in many shapes, sizes and speeds. **Zài Zhōngguó,** there are **pǔtōngchē,** *(poo-tohng-chuh)* ordinary trains
kuàichē *(kwhy-chuh)* fast trains **hé tèbié** *(tuh-bee-uh)* special **kuàichē.** *(kwhy-chuh)* fast trains Some **huǒchē yǒu** *(yoh)* have **cānchē.** *(tsahn-chuh)* dining car Some **huǒchē yǒu wòpù.** *(woh-poo)* sleeping car Some
huǒchē yǒu tǎngyǐ. *(tahng-yee)* reclining car All this will be indicated on the **shíjiān** *(shr-jee-ahn)* time **biǎo,** *(bee-ow)* schedule but remember, **nǐ zhīdào** *(jihr-dow)* know
zěnme *(zuhn-muh)* how **wèn** *(wuhn)* to ask **zhè xiē** *(juh) (ssee-eh)* these **wèntí.**

☐ **hǎo** *(how)* . . . . good _____
☐ **hǎochī** *(how-chr)* . . . . delicious _____
☐ **hǎochù** *(how-choo)* . . . . benefit 好 _____
☐ **hǎogǎn** *(how-gahn)* . . . . good impression _____
☐ **hǎoyì** *(how-yee)* . . . . goodwill *hǎo* _____

Knowing these travel **cí** will make your holiday twice as enjoyable and at least three times as easy. Review these **cí** by doing the crossword puzzle below. Drill yourself on this Step by selecting other destinations and ask your own **wèntí** about **huǒchē**, *(hwoh-chuh)* **gōnggòngqìchē** *(gohng-gohng-chee-chuh)* **huòzhě** **fēijī** *(fay-jee)* airplanes that go there. Select more **xīn cí** from your **cídiǎn** *(tsih-dee-ahn)* dictionary and practice asking **wèntí** beginning with **nǎr, shénme shíhou** and **duōshao qián**.

ACROSS
4. sleeping car
6. to book, reserve
7. to arrive, to
8. where
10. international
11. language
12. exit
14. pedicab
15. airport
19. train
20. main station
22. traveler, passenger
25. luggage, baggage
27. time schedule
28. very
29. counter

DOWN
1. documents
2. to pay
3. ticket
5. dining car
6. money-exchange office
7. map
9. entrance
12. compartment
13. emergency gate
14. lost-and-found office
16. passport
17. to know
18. airplane
21. to travel
23. fast
24. reclining car
26. boat

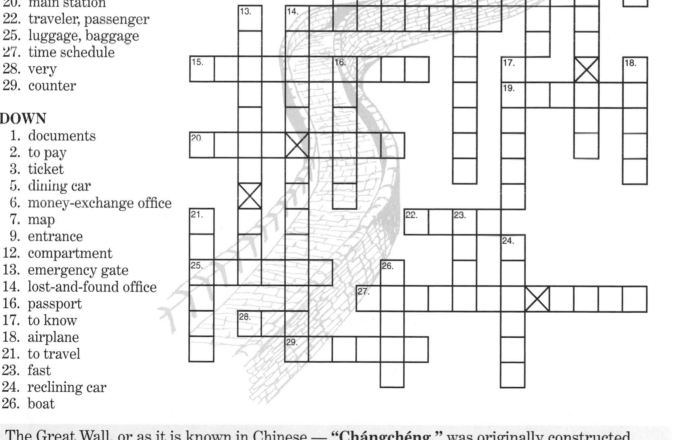

The Great Wall, or as it is known in Chinese — **"Chángchéng,"** was originally constructed during the Qin Dynasty (221-207 B.C.). Over time additional walls were linked to it. The estimates of its exact length range from 1,560 miles to over 3,000 miles.

❏ **hǎohàn** *(how-hahn)* . . . . wise man, hero _____
❏ **hǎotīng** *(how-teeng)* . . . . pleasant to the ear _____
❏ **hǎoxiào** *(how-ssee-ow)* . . . . funny _____
❏ **hǎokàn** *(how-kahn)* . . . . good-looking 好 _____
❏ **hǎoyùn** *(how-yoon)* . . . . good fortune *hǎo* _____

What about inquiring about *(jee-ah-chee-ahn)* **jiàqián?** prices   *(nung)* **Nǐ néng** can **wèn** ask **zhè ge wèntí.**

(tswong) **Cóng Shànghǎi** from *(dow)* **dào Běijīng** to *(dwoh-shao)* **duōshao** how much *(chee-ahn)* **qián?** money _____

(dahn-chuhng) **dānchéng** one-way _____

(lie-hway) **láihuí** round-trip _____

(dwoh-shao) *(chee-ahn)*
Cóng Shànghǎi dào Nánjīng duōshao qián? _____

(dahn-chuhng) *(hi-shr)* *(lie-hway)*
Dānchéng háishì láihuí? one-way / or / round-trip _____

(yeh) *(nung)* *(wuhn)* *(shun-muh)* *(shr-hoh)* *(ki)* *(dow)*
Nǐ yě néng wèn: also can ask **Shénme shíhou kāi?** what time depart   **Shénme shíhou dào?** arrive

(choo) *(hwoh-chuh)* *(ki)*
Qù Guǎngzhōu de huǒchē shénme shíhou kāi? to / train / departs _____

(fay-jee)
Qù Shànghǎi de fēijī shénme shíhou kāi? airplane _____

(dow)
Huǒchē shénme shíhou dào Xī'ān? arrives _____

Fēijī shénme shíhou dào Běijīng? _____

Nǐ have just arrived in **Zhōngguó. Xiànzài nǐ zài huǒchē** are (at) *(jahn)* **zhàn.** station **Nǐ** *(yow)* **yào** want *(choo)* **qù** to go to *(how)* **nǎr?** where **Hǎo,** well

tell that to the *(shoh-pee-ow-yoo-ahn)* **shòupiàoyuán** ticket seller at the *(gway-tie)* **guìtái.** counter

(ssee-ahng) *(choo)*
Wǒ xiǎng dào Hángzhōu qù. want / to / to go _____

(dow) *(chuh)* *(shr-hoh)* *(ki)*
Dào Hángzhōu de chē shénme shíhou kāi? to _____

(pee-ow) *(dwoh-shao)* *(chee-ahn)*
Dào Hángzhōu de piào duōshao qián? ticket / how much / money _____

(pee-ow)
Wǒ xiǎng yào yì zhāng piào. would like / (M) / ticket _____

ANSWERS

The answers are printed upside down.

ACROSS
4. wòpù
6. dǐng
7. dào
8. nǎr
10. guówài
11. huà
12. chūkǒu
14. sānlúnchē
15. fēijīchǎng
19. huǒchē
20. zǒng zhàn
22. lùkè

DOWN
1. wènjiān
2. fù qián
3. piào
5. cānchē
6. duìhuàn chù
7. dìtú
9. rùkǒu
12. chēxiāng
13. tàipíng mén
14. shíwù
16. huzhào
17. zhǐdào
18. fēijī
21. lǚxíng
23. kuài
24. tángyī
25. xíngli
26. chuán
27. shíjiān biǎo
28. hěn
29. guìtái

84

Xiànzài that **nǐ** know the words essential for traveling **zài Zhōngguó**, what are some specialty items **nǐ** might go in search of?

(sih)
sī
silk

(jee-nee-ahn-peen)
jìniànpǐn
souvenirs

(gohng-yee-peen)
gōngyìpǐn
artworks

(joo-bao)
zhūbǎo
jewelry

(dee-ow-kuh)
diāokè
carvings

(chah-joo)
chájù
tea service

Consider using CHINESE *a language map*® as well. CHINESE *a language map*® is the perfect companion for your travels when **nǐ** may not wish to take along this book. Each section focuses on essentials for your journey. Your *Language Map*® is not meant to replace learning

(jwong-wuhn)
Zhōngwén, but will help you in the event **nǐ** forget something and need a little bit of help. For more information, please turn to page 132 or go to www.bbks.com.

❏ **chá** *(chah)* . . . . tea
❏ **chábēi** *(chah-bay)* . . . . tea cup
❏ **chádiǎn** *(chah-dee-ahn)* . . . . light meal
❏ **cháguǎn** *(chah-gwahn)* . . . . teahouse
❏ **cháhuì** *(chah-hway)* . . . . tea party

chá

(tsi-dahn)
Càidān
menu

Xiànzài nǐ zài Zhōngguó de lǚguǎn le. *(loo-gwahn)* hotel **Nǐ** are hungry. **Nǐ xiǎng yào chīfàn.** *(chr-fahn)* to eat meal **Hǎo** *(how)* good

fànguǎn zài nǎr? First of all, **yǒu hěn duō chīfàn de dìfāng.** *(yoh)* there are *(huhn)* very *(dwoh)* many *(chr-fahn)* to eat meal *(dee-fahng)* places Let's learn them.

(loo-gwahn) *(chahn-teeng)*
lǚguǎn de chāntīng _____

a café in a hotel that serves a variety of **Zhōngguó**
as well as **Měiguó** dishes

(ssee-ow) *(chr-dee-ahn)*
xiǎo chīdiàn _____

a snack shop, usually open for breakfast, lunch and dinner

(mee-ahn) *(gwahn)*
miàn guǎn _____

a noodle shop that provides a variety of noodle dishes

(jee-oo) *(gwahn)*
jiǔ guǎn _____

a tavern that has a limited menu but some specialties

(fahn-gwahn)
fànguǎn _____

a restaurant that serves a variety of meals, depending upon
the province you are visiting

If **nǐ** look around you in a **Zhōngguó fànguǎn**, **nǐ** will see that **Zhōngguó rén** *(ruhn)* person uses two basic

eating utensils: ✕ **kuàizi** *(kwhy-zuh)* chopsticks and **tāngchí.** *(tahng-chr)* soup spoon Because all **Zhōngguó cài** *(tsi)* dishes are cut well, knives

are generally not used. Unlike **Měiguó** customs, bowls are brought to one's mouth when eating.

Before beginning your meal, you will say, "**chīfàn.**" *(chr-fahn)* let's eat Your turn to practice now.

_____
(Let's eat!)

And at least one more time for practice!

_____
(Let's eat!)

❏ **chájù** *(chah-joo)* .... tea service
❏ **cháshuǐ** *(chah-shway)* .... drink (tea, etc.)
❏ **cháyè** *(chah-yeh)* .... tea leaf
❏ **hóng chá** *(hohng)(chah)* .... black tea
❏ **lǜ chá** *(loo)(chah)* .... green tea

茶
chá _____

Start imagining now all the new taste treats you will experience abroad. Try all of the different

types of eating establishments mentioned on the previous page. Experiment. **Nǐ** may share a

(jwoh-zuh)
zhuōzi with others, which is a common and pleasant custom in **Zhōngguó.** If **nǐ kànjiàn** a vacant
table   *(kahn-jee-ahn)*
                                                                                        see

(yee-zuh)   *(jwoh-zuh)* *(ssee-ahn-shuhng)* *(juhr)* *(ruhn)*
yǐzi, just be sure to first ask those sitting at the **zhuōzi,** **"Xiānshēng, zhèr yǒu rén ma?"**
chair   sir   there has person

(ssee-oo-yow) *(tsi-dahn)*
If **nǐ xūyào yí ge càidān,** catch the attention
     need   menu
(foo-woo-yoo-uhn)
of the **fúwùyuán** saying,
        service person

(ssee-ahn-shuhng)   *(tsi-dahn)*
"Xiānshēng, qǐng gěi wǒ càidān."
                                        menu

_____

(Sir, please give me a menu.)

(tsi-dahn)   *(jihr-dow)*
Zhōngguó fànguǎn post their **càidān** outside. Always read it before entering so **nǐ zhīdào**
                                    menu   know
(jee-ah-chee-ahn)
what type of meals and **jiàqián** **nǐ** will encounter inside. Most **fànguǎn** will also write the
                         prices

special meal of the day on a blackboard just inside the **mén.** The meal of the day is always
                                                          (muhn)
                                                          door

seasonal and often consists of seafood or vegetables.

❐ **diàn** *(dee-ahn)* . . . . store, shop   _____
❐ **diànyuán** *(dee-ahn-yoo-ahn)* . . . . store clerk   _____
❐ **diànzhǔ** *(dee-ahn-joo)* . . . . storekeeper   店   _____
❐ **gǔdǒng diàn** *(goo-dwong)(dee-ahn)*. . . . . antique shop   _____
❐ **huā / huār diàn** *(hwah / hwahr)(dee-ahn)* . . . . florist shop   *diàn*

Zài Zhōngguó, yǒu *(yoh)* **sān ge** *(sahn)* **zhòngyàode** *(jwong-yow-duh)* meals to enjoy every day, plus **xiàwǔde** *(ssee-ah-woo-duh)* snacks **hé** *(afternoon)*

wǎnshàngde *(wahn-shahng-duh)* snacks.
(evening)

zǎofàn *(zow-fahn)* _____
(breakfast)

        Zài lǚguǎn, nǐ may eat **zǎofàn** between **liù diǎn** *(dee-ahn)* and **bā diǎn.**
                                                    (o'clock)

        Be sure to check the schedule before you retire for the night.

wǔfàn *(woo-fahn)* _____
(mid-day meal)

                     generally served from 11:30 to 14:30

wǎnfàn *(wahn-fahn)* _____
(evening meal)

         generally served from 18:00 to 20:30 and sometimes later;

              after 21:00, only snacks will be served.

Xiànzài, for a preview of delights to come . . . At the back of this **shū, nǐ** will find a sample

càidān. *(tsi-dahn)* Read it **jīntiān** *(jeen-tee-ahn)* and learn the **xīn cí.** When **nǐ** are ready to leave on your trip, cut out
(today)

the **càidān,** fold it, **hé** carry it in your pocket, wallet **huòzhě** purse. Before you go, how do **nǐ** say

these **sān** phrases which are so very important for the hungry traveler?

Sir, is this space vacant (is there a person here)? _____

Sir, please give me a menu. _____

Let's eat! _____

_____ **chī** *(chr)* **yú?** *(yoo)*   _____ **hē** *(huh)* **jiǔ?** *(jee-oo)*
(who) eats fish   *(who)* drinks

_____ (who)

_____ **lǚxíng dào** *(dow)* **Shànghǎi?**
(who)   to

❐ **lǐfà diàn** *(lee-fah)(dee-ahn)* . . . . hairdressers
❐ **ròu diàn** *(roh)(dee-ahn)* . . . . butcher shop
❐ **shū diàn** *(shoo)(dee-ahn)* . . . . bookstore
❐ **yào diàn** *(yow)(dee-ahn)* . . . . pharmacy
❐ **xié diàn** *(ssee-eh)(dee-ahn)* . . . . shoe store

店
diàn

_____
_____
_____
_____
_____

(tsi-dahn)

Càidān below has the main categories **nǐ** will find in most restaurants. Learn them **jīntiān** so that **nǐ** will easily recognize them when you dine **zài Zhōngguó.** Be sure to write the words in the blanks below.

(tsi-dahn)
Càidān

(lung-pahn)
lěngpán
appetizers

(shway-gwoh)
shuǐguǒ
fruit

(tahng)
tāng
soups

(cheeng-tsi)
qīngcài
green vegetables

(dahn)
dàn
eggs

(yah)
yā
duck

(mee-ahn) (fahn)
miàn fàn
noodles and rice

(joo)
jī
chicken

(hi-ssee-ahn)
hǎixiān
seafood

(tee-ahn-dee-ahn)
tiándiǎn
dessert

(nee-oo-roh)
niúròu
beef

(joo-roh)
zhūròu
pork

(yeen-lee-ow)
yǐnliào
beverages

Learning the following should help you to identify what kind of meat **nǐ** have ordered and **zěnme** it will be prepared.

- ❏ **niúròu** *(nee-oo-roh)* . . . . beef _____
- ❏ **jī** *(jee)* . . . . chicken _____
- ❏ **zhūròu** *(joo-roh)* . . . . pork _____
- ❏ **yángròu** *(yahng-roh)* . . . . mutton _____

89

Nǐ néng *(nung)* *(can)* generally order **qīngcài** *(cheeng-tsi)* *(green vegetables)* with your meal, as well as **miàn** *(mee-ahn)* *(noodles)* or **fàn**. *(fahn)* *(rice)* One **tiān** at a **càichǎng** *(tsi-chahng)* *(market)* will teach **nǐ** the **míngzì** of different kinds of **cài** *(tsi)* *(vegetables)* **hé shuǐguǒ,** *(shway-gwoh)* *(fruit)* plus it will be a delightful experience for **nǐ**. **Nǐ néng** *(nung)* always consult your menu guide at the back of this **shū** if **nǐ** forget the **zhèngquède míngzì**. *(jung-choo-eh-duh)* *(correct)* **Xiànzài nǐ** have decided what **nǐ xiǎng yào** *(would like)* **chī** *(chr)* *(to eat)* and **fúwùyuán** *(foo-woo-yoo-ahn)* *(service person)* **lái le**. *(lie)* *(comes)*

Don't forget that **Zhōngguó** dishes are regional and that various provinces have their own specialties. **Nǐ** would not want to miss out on the following specialties.

zòngzi *(zwong-zuh)*
stuffed sweet rice wrapped with bamboo leaves

tāngyuán *(tahng-yoo-ahn)*
sweet rice-flour ball

chūnjuǎn *(choon-joo-ahn)*
pastry filled with a savory mixture of vegetables and meat (spring roll)

xiāròu hún tūn *(ssee-ah-roh) (hoon) (toon)*
shrimp and vegetables in a wrapper, boiled

Most **fànguǎn** also offer **náshǒucài,** *(nah-shoh-tsi)* which are the chef's special dishes. Because it is a custom in **Zhōngguó** to share all the dishes which one's party has ordered, make sure you know the size of the dish before you order it. The dishes will be marked in the **càidān** *(tsi-dahn)* as

Small 小   Medium 中   Large 大

☐ **yā** *(yah)* . . . . duck _____

☐ **yú** *(yoo)* . . . . fish _____

☐ **jīdàn** *(jee-dahn)* . . . . eggs _____

☐ **zhà** *(jah)* . . . . deep-fried _____

☐ **shāo** *(shao)* . . . . roasted _____

(juhr)
Zhèr shì (this) an example of what **nǐ** might select for your evening meal. Using your menu guide on pages 117 and 118, as well as what **nǐ** have learned in this Step, fill in the blanks *in English* with what **nǐ** believe your **fúwùyuán** *(foo-woo-yoo-ahn)* will bring you. The answers **zài xiàbiān.** *(ssee-ah-bee-ahn)*

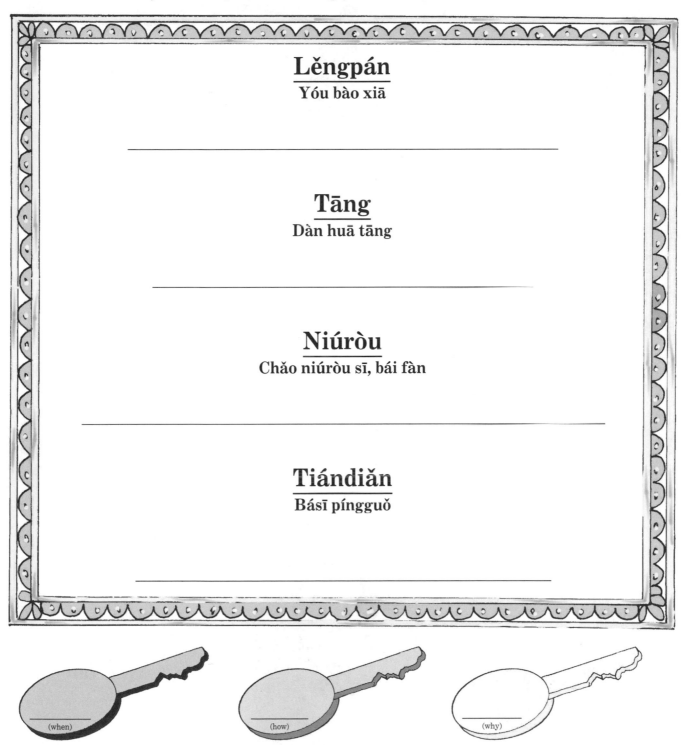

Lěngpán

Yóu bào xiā

____

Tāng

Dàn huā tāng

____

Niúròu

Chǎo niúròu sī, bái fàn

____

Tiándiǎn

Básī píngguǒ

____

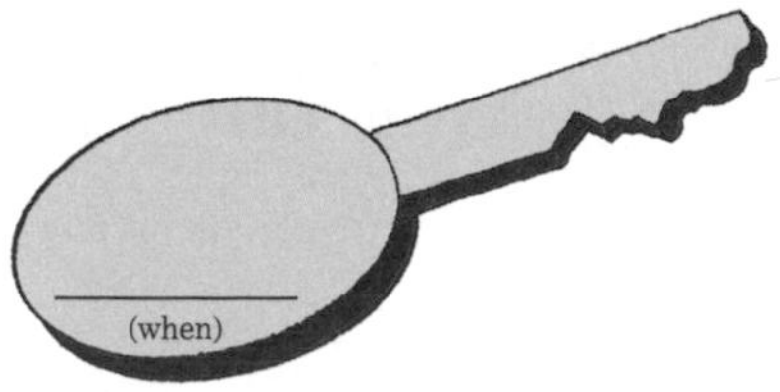

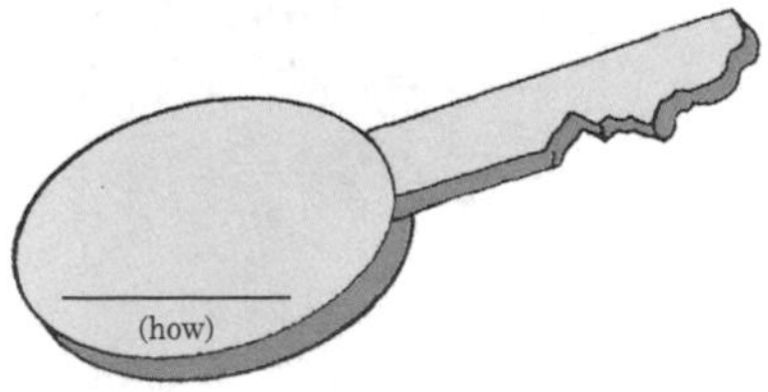

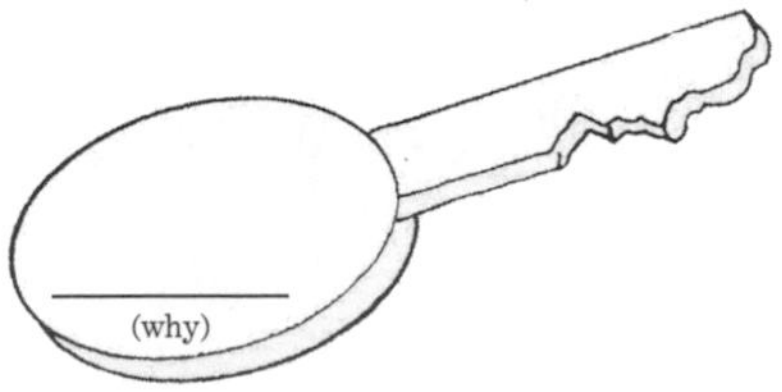

ANSWERS

Appetizer:	**Oil-fried shrimp**
Soup:	**Egg-flower soup**
Beef:	**Stir-fried beef, plain rice**
Dessert:	**Hot-candied apple**

Xiànzài is a good time for a quick review. Draw lines between the matching **Yīngwén** and

Zhōngwén cí below.

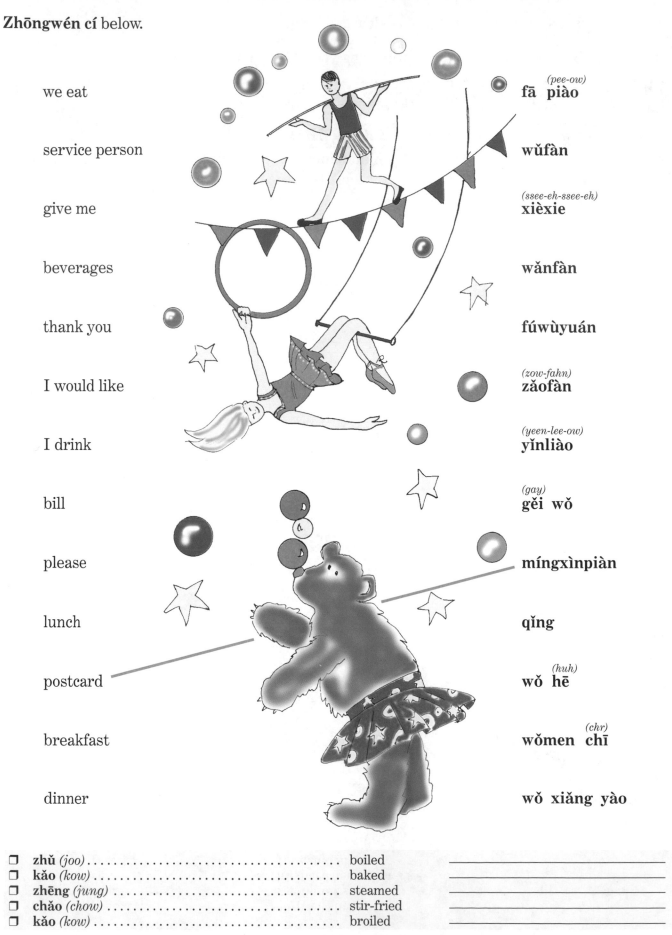

we eat	**fā piào** *(pee-ow)*
service person	**wǔfàn**
give me	**xièxie** *(ssee-eh-ssee-eh)*
beverages	**wǎnfàn**
thank you	**fúwùyuán**
I would like	**zǎofàn** *(zow-fahn)*
I drink	**yǐnliào** *(yeen-lee-ow)*
bill	**gěi wǒ** *(gay)*
please	**míngxìnpiàn**
lunch	**qǐng**
postcard	**wǒ hē** *(huh)*
breakfast	**wǒmen chī** *(chr)*
dinner	**wǒ xiǎng yào**

❏ **zhǔ** *(joo)* . . . . boiled   _____
❏ **kǎo** *(kow)* . . . . baked   _____
❏ **zhēng** *(jung)* . . . . steamed   _____
❏ **chǎo** *(chow)* . . . . stir-fried   _____
❏ **kǎo** *(kow)* . . . . broiled   _____

(dee-ahn-hwah)
Diànhuà
telephone

Zài Zhōngguó, what is different about the *(dee-ahn-hwah)* **diànhuà?** Well, **nǐ** never notice such things until **nǐ**

want to use them. **Diànhuà** allow you to make reservations for a **lǔguǎn,** *(my)* **mǎi** *(ssee-pee-ow)* **xìpiào** **hé**
　　　　　　　　　　　　　　　　　　　　　　　　　　　　　　hotel　　buy　theater tickets

(fay-jee-pee-ow) *(nee-duh)* *(pung-yoh)* *(choo-zoo-chuh)*
fēijīpiào, contact **nǐde** **péngyou,** check on the hours of a **bówùguǎn,** call a **chūzūchē,** make
airplane tickets　　your　friends　　　　　　　　　　　museum

emergency calls and a lot of other things that **wǒmen** do *(tee-ahn-tee-ahn)* **tiāntiān.** It also gives you a certain
　　　　　　　　　　　　　　　　　　　　　　　　　everyday

amount of freedom when **nǐ** can make your own calls.

Depending upon where your travels take you, **nǐ** may need to find a *(gohng-yohng)* **gōngyòng diànhuà.**
　　　　　　　　　　　　　　　　　　　　　　　　　　　　　public

(yoh-joo) *(gohng-yohng)* *(fay-jee-chahng)*
Zài yóujú **yǒu** **gōngyòng diànhuà.** **Fēijīchǎng**
post office　there are　public　　　　　　　airports

hé the large shopping centers also **yǒu**

diànhuà tíng.
booths

So, let's learn *(zuhn-muh)* **zěnme** to operate the
　　　　　　　　how

diànhuà. Many **diànhuà** use **diànhuà**
　　　　　　　　　　　　　telephone

(kah) *(nung)*
kǎ. Nǐ néng buy these at the post office.
cards　can

Another option is to purchase a local

SIM card for your cell phone.

Well, before you turn the page it would be a

good idea to go back and review all your

numbers one more time.

To dial from the United States to most other countries **nǐ** need that country's international area

code. Your **diànhuà** *(boo)* **bù** at home should have a listing of international area codes.
telephone book

Zhèr shì some very useful words built around the word "**diànhuà.**"
- ❏ **gōngyòng diànhuà** *(gohng-yohng)(dee-ahn-hwah)* ...... public telephone _____
- ❏ **diànhuà tíng** *(dee-ahn-hwah)(teeng)* .... telephone booth _____
- ❏ **diànhuà bù** *(dee-ahn-hwah)(boo)* .... telephone book _____
- ❏ **běndì diànhuà** *(buhn-dee)(dee-ahn-hwah)* .... local telephone call _____

When **nǐ** leave your contact numbers with friends, family **hé** business colleagues, **nǐ** should include your destination's country code **hé** city code whenever possible . For example,

City Codes		City Codes	
Quǎngzhōu	20	Běijīng	10
Xī'ān	29	Shànghǎi	21
Wūlǔmùqí	991	Tiānjīn	22
Hángzhōu	571	Kūnmíng	871
Wǔhàn	27	Lāsà	891

The country code for **Zhōngguó** is — 86 —

To call from one city to another **zài Zhōngguó, nǐ** may place it through your **lǔguǎn** service desk or by using a **diànhuà** *(kah)* **kǎ** in a special card telephone. **Nǐ** can say: "**Wǒ xiǎng yào dǎ diànhuà** *(dow)* **dào Běijīng.**" or "**Wǒ xiǎng yào dǎ diànhuà dào Nánjīng.**"
telephone   card   make

Now you try it: _____

(I would like to call to . . .)

When answering the **diànhuà, nǐ** pick up the *(teeng-tohng)* **tīngtǒng** and say,
receiver

(way)   *(neen-how)*
"**Wèi. Nínhǎo.**"
hey   hello

Zhōngguó rén usually say, "*(zi-jee-ahn)* **Zàijiàn,**" when ending a **diànhuàde** *(dee-ahn-hwah-duh)* **duìhuà** *(dway-hwah)* even though it
good-bye   conversation

actually means "see you again." Your turn – _____

(good-bye)

Also, if **nǐ** are told "*(yoh)* **Yǒu** *(ruhn)* **rén** *(shwoh-hwah)* **shuōhuà,**" don't be surprised — it simply means the line is occupied.
there is   person   speaking

Don't forget that **nǐ** *(nung)* **néng** ask . . .
can

(chahng-too)   *(dow)*
Dǎ chángtú diànhuà dào Měiguó duōshao qián? _____
make   long-distance   to   U.S.A.

(jee-ah-nah-dah)
Dǎ chángtú diànhuà dào Jiānádà duōshao qián? _____
Canada

Zhèr shì some emergency telephone numbers.
- ❑ **jǐngchá** *(jeeng-chah)* .... police   110 _____
- ❑ **huǒ** *(hwoh)* .... fire   119 _____
- ❑ **běndì cháhàotái** *(buhn-dee)(chah-how-tie)* .... local directory assistance   114 _____
- ❑ **chángtú cháhàotái** *(chahng-too)(chah-how-tie)* .... long-distance assistance   113 _____

Zhèr shì some sample sentences for the **diànhuà.** Write them in the blanks to the right.

Wǒ xiǎng yào dǎ diànhuà dào San Francisco. _____

Wǒ xiǎng yào dǎ diànhuà dào fēijīchǎng. _(fay-jee-chahng)_ airport _____

Wǒ xiǎng yào dǎ diànhuà dào "Jīn Hǎi Fànguǎn." _(jeen)_ _(hi)_ golden sea _____

(woh-duh)
Wǒde diànhuà shì Běijīng, 6765-8974. my _____

(nee-duh) _(how)_
Nǐde diànhuà duōshao hào? your number _____

Lǚguǎn diànhuà duōshao hào? _____

Christina: _(way)_ _(neen-how)_ _(jee-ow)_
Wèi. Nínhǎo. Qǐng jiào Lǐ Sǐ tīng diànhuà.
call listen to

_____

Operator: _(yoh)_ _(ruhn)_ _(shwoh-hwah)_
Yǒu rén shuōhuà.

_____

Christina: _(jihr)_ _(mahn)_ _(mahn)_
Wǒ zhǐ shuō yìdiǎn Zhōngwén. Qǐng nǐ màn man shuō.
only a little slowly

_____

Operator: **Duìbùqǐ. Yǒu rén shuōhuà.**

_____

Christina: _(zi-jee-ahn)_
Xièxie. Zàijiàn.

When speaking to someone in a foreign language, it is most helpful if you look at the person,

speak **hěn** slowly and distinctly. **Nǐ** don't need to raise your voice, just speak clearly.

Zhèr shì countries **nǐ** may wish to call.
- ❏ **Áodàlìyá** _(ow-dah-lee-yah)_ .... Australia _____
- ❏ **Āodìlì** _(ow-dee-lee)_ .... Austria _____
- ❏ **Bǐlìshí** _(bee-lee-shr)_ .... Belgium _____
- ❏ **Jiānádà** _(jee-ah-nah-dah)_ .... Canada _____

95

An excellent means of transportation is the **dìtiě**. *(dee-tee-eh)* subway However, many **Zhōngguó rén** travel by

(dee-ahn-chuh) *(gohng-gohng-chee-chuh)* *(chahng-chahng)*
diànchē **huòzhě gōnggòngqìchē. Zài Zhōngguó, gōnggòngqìchē** are **chángcháng** very
trolley often

crowded. Let's learn how to take the **gōnggòngqìchē**, *(gohng-gohng-chee-chuh)* **dìtiě** *(dee-tee-eh)* subway **huòzhě diànchē**. *(dee-ahn-chuh)* trolley

(dee-tee-eh)
dìtiě
subway

(gohng-gohng-chee-chuh)
gōnggòngqìchē
bus

(dee-tee-eh) *(jahn)*
dìtiě **zhàn**
subway stop

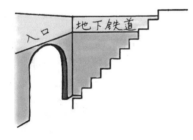

(dee-ahn-chuh)
diànchē
trolley

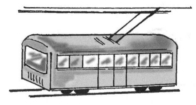

(gohng-gohng-chee-chuh) *(jahn)*
gōnggòngqìchē **zhàn**
bus stop

(dee-too)
Dìtú displaying the various **chē** *(chuh)* **zhàn** *(jahn)* **hé** **lù** *(loo)* are available at most major stops. Be sure to let
maps stops routes

(shoh-pee-ow-yoo-ahn)
the **shòupiàoyuán** know where **nǐ** are going, because ticket prices are based on distances
conductor

traveled. This applies to both **gōnggòngqìchē** *(gohng-gohng-chee-chuh)* and **diànchē**. *(dee-ahn-chuh)* Consider buying a **yīkǎtōng**, *(yee-kah-tong)* one-card pass

(bay-jeeng)
which is a transportation smart card for **Běijīng**.

❑ **Déguó** *(duh-gwoh)* . . . . Germany _____
❑ **Yīngguó** *(yeeng-gwoh)* . . . . England _____
❑ **Xībānyá** *(ssee-bahn-yah)* . . . . Spain _____
❑ **Fǎguó** *(fah-gwoh)* . . . . France _____
❑ **Yìdàlì** *(yee-dah-lee)* . . . . Italy _____

Other than having foreign words, the **dìtiě** *(dee-tee-eh)* functions just like the one in London **huòzhě** New York. Locate your destination, select the correct line on your practice **dìtiě** and hop on board.

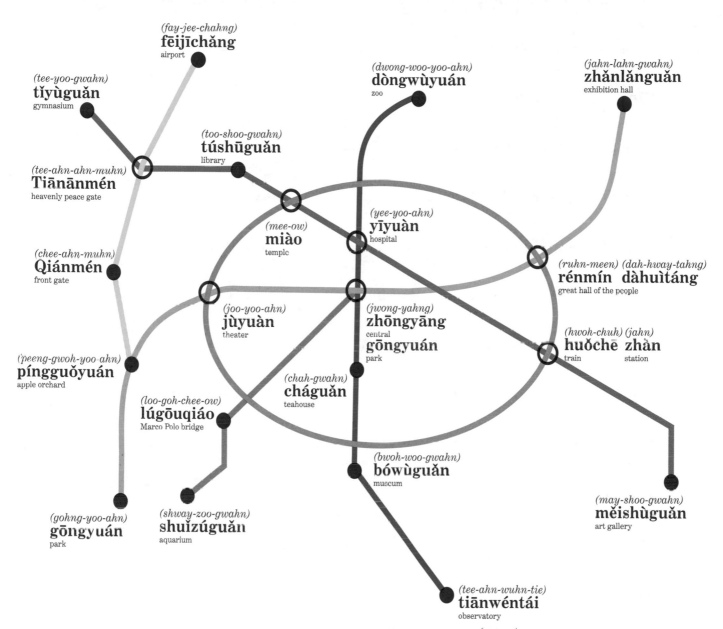

(fay-jee-chahng) **fēijīchǎng** airport

(tee-yoo-gwahn) **tǐyùguǎn** gymnasium

(too-shoo-gwahn) **túshūguǎn** library

(tee-ahn-ahn-muhn) **Tiānānmén** heavenly peace gate

(chee-ahn-muhn) **Qiánmén** front gate

(peeng-gwoh-yoo-ahn) **píngguǒyuán** apple orchard

(loo-goh-chee-ow) **lúgōuqiáo** Marco Polo bridge

(gohng-yoo-ahn) **gōngyuán** park

(shway-zoo-gwahn) **shuǐzúguǎn** aquarium

(mee-ow) **miào** temple

(joo-yoo-ahn) **jùyuàn** theater

(chah-gwahn) **cháguǎn** teahouse

(dwong-woo-yoo-ahn) **dòngwùyuán** zoo

(yee-yoo-ahn) **yīyuàn** hospital

(jwong-yahng) **zhōngyāng** central *(gohng-yoo-ahn)* **gōngyuán** park

(bwoh-woo-gwahn) **bówùguǎn** museum

(tee-ahn-wuhn-tie) **tiānwéntái** observatory

(jahn-lahn-gwahn) **zhǎnlǎnguǎn** exhibition hall

(ruhn-meen) *(dah-hway-tahng)* **rénmín dàhuìtáng** great hall of the people

(hwoh-chuh) *(jahn)* **huǒchē zhàn** train station

(may-shoo-gwahn) **měishùguǎn** art gallery

Say these questions aloud many times and don't forget you need a **piào**! *(pee-ow)* ticket

(nahr) *(shr)* *(gohng-gohng-chee-chuh)* *(jahn)*
Nǎr shì gōnggòngqìchē zhàn?
where is — stop

(dee-ahn-chuh)
Nǎr shì diànchē zhàn?

(dee-tee-eh)
Nǎr shì dìtiě zhàn?

(choo-zoo-chuh)
Nǎr shì chūzūchē zhàn?
taxi

- ❐ **Xīnxīlán** *(sseen-ssee-lahn)* .... New Zealand _____
- ❐ **Nánfēi** *(nahn-fay)* .... South Africa _____
- ❐ **Yìndù** *(yeen-doo)* .... India _____
- ❐ **Rìběn** *(ree-buhn)* .... Japan _____
- ❐ **Ruìshì** *(rway-shr)* .... Switzerland _____

Practice the following basic **wèntí** *(questions)* out loud and then **xiě** *(ssee-eh)* *(write)* them in the blanks **zài yòubiān.** *(yoh-bee-ahn)* *(right side)*

1. **Gōnggòngqìchē shénme** *(shun-muh)* *(what)* **shíhou** *(shr-hoh)* *(time / when)* **dào?** *(dow)* *(arrives)* _____

    Diànchē shénme shíhou dào? _____

    (dee-tee-eh)
    Dìtiě shénme shíhou dào? _____

2. **Gōnggòngqìchē shénme shíhou kāi?** *(ki)* *(leaves)* _____

    Diànchē shénme shíhou kāi? _____

    (dee-tee-eh)
    Dìtiě shénme shíhou kāi? _____

3. **Gōnggòngqìchē dào bówùguǎn duōshao** *(dwoh-shao)* *(how much)* **qián?** *(chee-ahn)* *(money)* _____

    Diànchē dào dòngwùyuán *(dwong-woo-yoo-ahn)* *(zoo)* **duōshao qián?** _____

    Dìtiě dào lǚguǎn duōshao qián? _____

4. **Gōnggòngqìchē zhàn** *(jahn)* *(stop)* **zài** *(zi)* *(is)* **nǎr?** *(where)* _____

    Diànchē zhàn zài nǎr? _____

    (dee-tee-eh)
    Dìtiě zhàn zài nǎr? _____

Let's change directions and learn these **xīn dòngcí.** **Nǐ** know the basic "plug-in" formula, so write out your own sentences using these new verbs.

xǐ *(ssee)* *(to wash)* _____

diū *(dee-oo)* *(to lose)* _____

yào *(yow)* *(to want)* _____

Zhèr shì a few holidays which you might experience during your visit.

- ❏ **chūnjié** *(choon-jee-eh)* . . . . Chinese New Year
- ❏ **wǔyī láodòng jié** *(woo-yee)(lao-dohng)(jee-eh)* . . . . Labor Day (May 1)
- ❏ **guóqìng jié** *(gwoh-cheeng)(jee-eh)* . . . . National Day (October 1)
- ❏ **liùyī értóng jié** *(lee-oo-yee)(ur-tohng)(jee-eh)* . . . . Children's Day (June 1)

(my) *(my)*
Mǎi hé Mài
to buy   to sell

(why-gwoh)
Zài wàiguó, shopping is **hěn yǒuyìsi.** The simple everyday task of buying **yì píng niúnǎi**
foreign country   very   interesting   *(peeng)* *(nee-oo-ni)* bottle   milk

(peeng-gwoh)
huòzhě yí ge píngguǒ becomes a challenge that **nǐ xiànzài** should be able to meet easily. Of
apple

(my) *(jee-nee-ahn-peen)* *(yoh-pee-ow)* *(meeng-sseen-pee-ahn)*
course, **nǐ** will **mǎi jìniànpǐn, yóupiào hé míngxìnpiàn,** but do not forget those many other
buy   souvenirs   stamps

(dwong-ssee) *(ah-sih-pee-leen)*
dōngxi ranging from shoelaces to **āsīpǐlín** that **nǐ** might need unexpectedly. Locate your
things   aspirin

store, draw a line to it and, as always, write your new words in the blanks provided.

(by-hwoh)
bǎihuò diàn _____
department   store

(dee-ahn-yeeng-yoo-ahn)
diànyǐngyuàn _____
movie theater

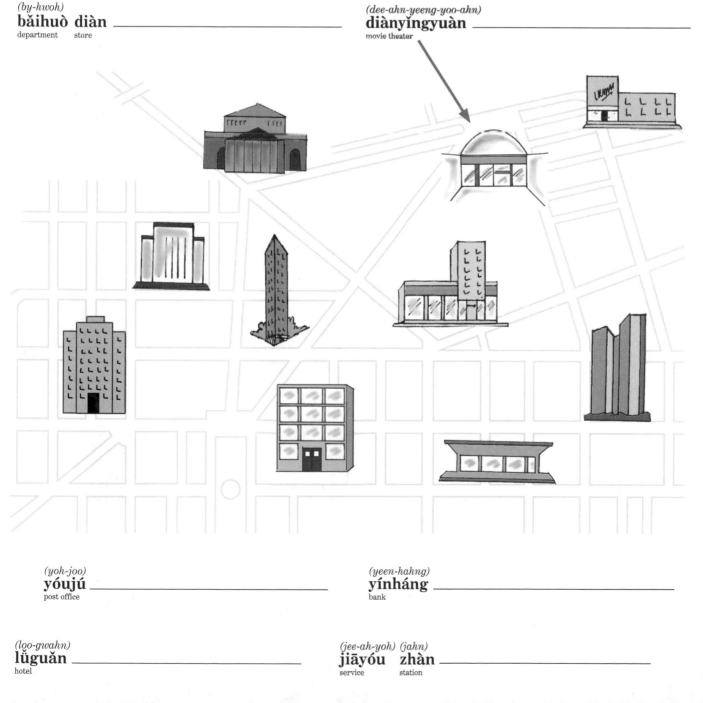

(yoh-joo)
yóujú _____
post office

(yeen-hahng)
yínháng _____
bank

(loo-gwahn)
lǚguǎn _____
hotel

(jee-ah-yoh) *(jahn)*
jiāyóu zhàn _____
service   station

(shahng-dee-ahn)
Shāngdiàn are open **qī** **tiān** per **xīngqī.**
shops
(chee)
seven
(sseeng-chee)
week

(shr-jee-ahn-bee-ow)
Of course, **shíjiānbiǎo** vary from
hours

shāngdiàn to **shāngdiàn.**

(roh)
ròu diàn
butcher shop

_____

(shoo-dee-ahn)
shūdiàn
bookstore

_____

_____ *(gahn-ssee)*
gānxǐ diàn
dry cleaners

_____ *(shoo-shr)*
shúshí diàn
delicatessen

_____ *(yow) (dee-ahn)*
yào diàn
pharmacy

_____ *(teeng-chuh) (chahng)*
tíngchē chǎng
parking lot

tíngchē chǎng

_____ *(shoo-bao) (tahn)*
shūbào tān
bookstand

_____ *(shr-peen) (dee-ahn)*
shípǐn diàn
grocery store

_____ *(dee-ahn-chee)*
diànqì diàn
electronics   store

Make a list **xiànzài** of the **dōngxi nǐ** might

wish to purchase, pull out your **cídiǎn** and

prepare a shopping list in **Zhōngwén** for

your upcoming journey.

(loo-sseeng) (shuh)
lǚxíng shè
travel   agency

_____

(goo-dwong)
gǔdǒng diàn
antique   store

_____

(nee-oo-ni) (dee-ahn)
niúnǎi diàn
dairy

(hwahr)
huār diàn
flower   shop

(yoo) (dee-ahn)
yú diàn
fish   shop

_____   _____

(shway-gwoh)
shuǐguǒ diàn
fruit

(tsi-chahng)
càichǎng   *càichǎng, càichǎng*
market

(jee-nee-ahn-peen)
jìniànpǐn diàn
souvenir

(jwong-bee-ow)
zhōngbiǎo diàn
watchmakers

(mee-ahn-bao) (dee-ahn)
miànbāo diàn
bakery

(kah-fay) (gwahn)
kāfēi guǎn
coffee   shop

(ssee-yee)
xǐyī diàn
laundry

(wuhn-joo)
wénjù diàn
stationery   store

(lee-fah)
lǐfà diàn
hairdressers

ground (first) floor =	**yī lóu** *(loh)*	
second floor =	**èr lóu** *(ur)*	
third floor =	**sān lóu**	

(by-hwoh) *(dee-ahn)*
Bǎihuò Diàn
department   store

At this point, **nǐ** should just about be ready for **nǐde** *(nee-duh)* **Zhōngguó** *(loo-sseeng)* **lǚxíng. Nǐ** have gone

shopping for those last-minute odds 'n ends. Most likely, the store directory at your local

(by-hwoh) **bǎihuò diàn** did not look like the one **xiàbiān! Nǐ zhīdào** that *(noo-ruhn)* **"nǚrén" shì Zhōngwén** for
department   store   know

(ssee-oo-yow)
"women" so if **nǐ xūyào** something for a **nǚren, nǐ** would probably look on which floor?
          need

5	楼	yínqì diànqì bōlí shíwù	银器 电器 玻璃 食物	(silver) (electronics) (glassware) (food)
4	楼	shū wénjù wánjù jiājù	书籍 文具 玩具 家俱	(books) (stationery) (toys) (furniture)
3	楼	nánzhuāng nǚzhuāng gùkè fúwù	男装 女装 顾客服务台	(men's clothing) (women's clothing) (customer service)
2	楼	xié gōngjù yùndòng yòngpǐn	鞋 工具 运动用品	(shoes) (tools) (sporting goods)
1	楼	zhàoxiàng yòngpǐn zhūbǎo pízhì pǐn zhōngbiǎo	照相用品 珠宝 皮制品 钟表	(cameras) (jewelry) (leather) (clocks & watches)

(yee-foo) *(hi)* *(ssee-oo-yow)* *(shun-muh)*
Let's start a checklist for **nǐde lǚxíng.** Besides **yīfu, nǐ hái xūyào** to buy **shénme?** As
        clothes   still   need   what

(chee-ahng-jee-ow)
you learn these **cí** assemble these items **zài qiángjiǎo** of your **fángzi.** Check and make sure
                corner

that they are clean and ready for **nǐde lǚxíng.** On the next pages, match each item to its picture,

draw a line to it and write out the word many times. As **nǐ** organize these things, check them off

on this list. Do not forget to take the next group of sticky labels and label these **dōngxi** today.

(hoo-jow)
hùzhào
passport

(fay-jee-pee-ow)
fēijīpiào
airline ticket

(ssee-ahng-zuh)
xiāngzi
suitcase

xiāngzi, xiāngzi, xiāngzi ✔

(pee-bao)
píbāo
purse / handbag

(pee-jee-ah-zuh)
píjiāzi
wallet

(chee-ahn)
qián
money

(sseen-yohng-kah)
xìnyòngkǎ
credit cards

(loo-sseeng) *(jihr-pee-ow)*
lǚxíng **zhīpiào**
traveler's checks

(jow-ssee-ahng-jee)
zhàoxiàngjī
camera

(jee-ow-joo-ahn)
jiāojuǎn
film

(yoh-yohng-yee)
yóuyǒngyī
swimsuit

(yoh-yohng-yee)
yóuyǒngyī
swimsuit

(lee-ahng-ssee-eh)
liángxié
sandals

(tie-yahng) *(yahn-jeeng)*
tàiyáng yǎnjìng
sunglasses

(yah-shwah)
yáshuā
toothbrush

(yah-gow)
yágāo
toothpaste

(fay-zow)
féizào
soap

(gwah-lee-ahn-dow)
guāliǎndāo
razor

(choo-hahn-jee)
chúhànjì
deodorant

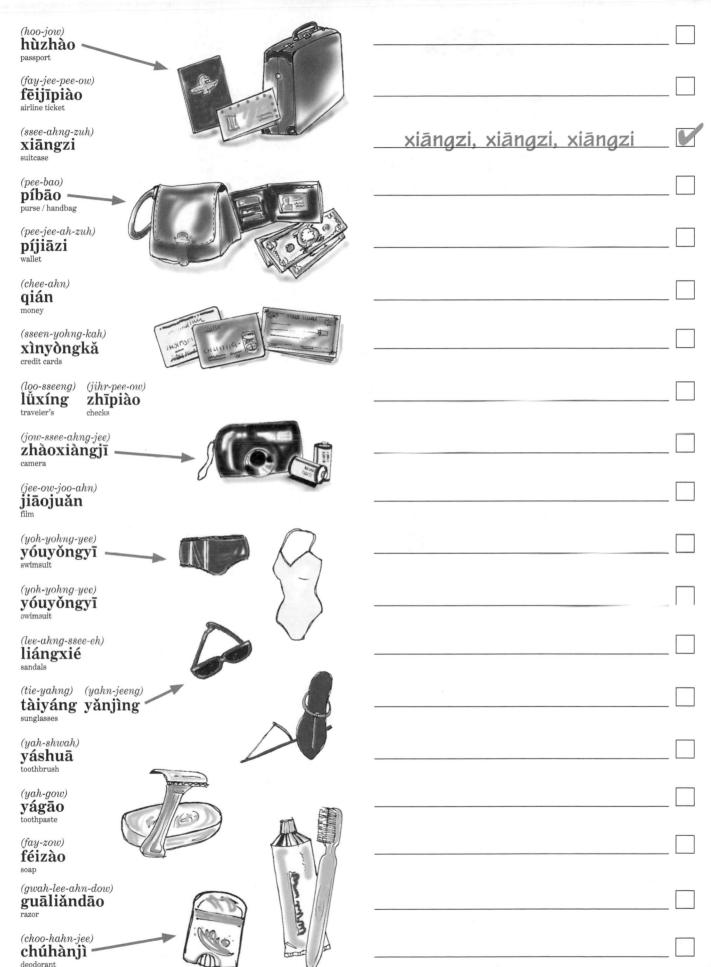

(shoo-zuh)
shūzi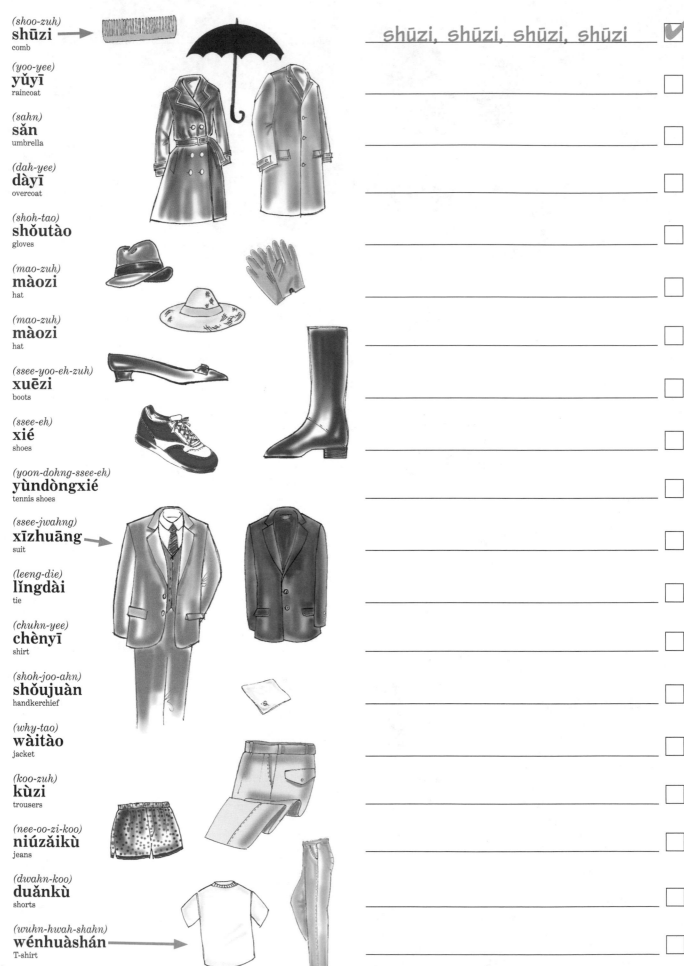
comb

shūzi, shūzi, shūzi, shūzi ✔

(yoo-yee)
yǔyī
raincoat

(sahn)
sǎn
umbrella

(dah-yee)
dàyī
overcoat

(shoh-tao)
shǒutào
gloves

(mao-zuh)
màozi
hat

(mao-zuh)
màozi
hat

(ssee-yoo-eh-zuh)
xuēzi
boots

(ssee-eh)
xié
shoes

(yoon-dohng-ssee-eh)
yùndòngxié
tennis shoes

(ssee-jwahng)
xīzhuāng
suit

(leeng-die)
lǐngdài
tie

(chuhn-yee)
chènyī
shirt

(shoh-joo-ahn)
shǒujuàn
handkerchief

(why-tao)
wàitào
jacket

(koo-zuh)
kùzi
trousers

(nee-oo-zi-koo)
niúzǎikù
jeans

(dwahn-koo)
duǎnkù
shorts

(wuhn-hwah-shahn)
wénhuàshán
T-shirt

104

(nay-koo)
nèikù
underpants

(nay-yee)
nèiyī
undershirt

(lee-ahn-yee-choon)
liányīqún
dress

(chuhn-yee)
chènyī
blouse

(choon-zuh)
qúnzi
skirt

___qúnzi, qúnzi, qúnzi, qúnzi___ ✔

(mao-yee)
máoyī
sweater

(chuhn-choon)
chènqún
slip

(ssee-wong-jow)
xiōngzhào
bra

(nay-koo)
nèikù
underpants

(wah-zuh)
wàzi
socks

(koo-wah)
kùwà
pantyhose

(shway-yee)
shuìyī
pajamas

(shway-yee)
shuìyī
nightshirt

(shway-pow)
shuìpáo
bathrobe

(twoh-ssee-eh)
tuōxié
slippers

From now on, **nǐ** *(yoh)* **yǒu** " *(fay-zow)* **féizào**" and not "soap." Having assembled these **dōngxi, nǐ** are ready
have   things

for **nǐde lǚxíng.** Let's add these important shopping phrases to your basic repertoire.
your

Shénme *(chee-tsoon)* **chǐcùn?** _____
what   measurement (what size)

(shr-huh)
Shìhé. _____
it fits

(boo) (shr-huh)
Bú shìhé. _____
it does not fit

105

Treat yourself to a final review. **Nǐ** know the **míngzì** for **Zhōngguó shāngdiàn** *(shahng-dee-ahn)*, so let's practice
names
shopping. Just remember your key question **cí** that you learned in Step 2. Whether **nǐ** need to

buy a **màozi** *(mao-zuh)* **huòzhě** a **shū** the necessary **cí** are the same.
or

1.   First step — **nǎr?**

Yào diàn zài nǎr? *(yow) (dee-ahn)*
pharmacy

Yínháng zài nǎr?
bank

Diànyǐngyuàn zài nǎr? *(dee-ahn-yeeng-yoo-ahn)*
movie theater

Bǎihuò diàn zài nǎr? *(by-hwoh)*
department

_____
(Where is the bakery?)

_____
(Where is the grocery store?)

_____
(Where is the market?)

2.   Second step — tell them what **nǐ xūyào** *(ssee-oo-yow)* **huòzhě xiǎng** *(ssee-ahng)* **yào!** *(yow)*
need   would like

Wǒ xūyào . . . *(ssee-oo-yow)*
I   need

Wǒ xiǎng yào . . .
I   would like

Nǐmen yǒu . . . ma? *(yoh)*
do you have

_____
(Do you have postcards?)

_____
(I would like four stamps.)

_____
(I need toothpaste.)

_____
(I need film.)

_____
(Do you have coffee?)

Go through the glossary at the end of this **shū** and select **èrshí ge cí**. *(ur-shr)* Drill the above patterns twenty with **zhè èrshí ge cí**. Don't cheat. Drill them **jīntiān**. *(jeen-tee-ahn)* **Xiànzài,** take **èrshí ge cí** more from

(nee-duh) *(tsih-dee-ahn)*
nǐde cídiǎn and do the same.
your dictionary

3. Third step — find out **duōshao qián.**
(dwoh-shao) *(chee-ahn)*
how much money

(nah)
Nà ge duōshao?   **Nà ge duōshao qián?**   **Qiānbǐ duōshao qián?** *(chee-ahn-bee)*
that   pencil

_____
(How much does the toothpaste cost?)

_____
(How much does the soap cost?)

_____
(How much does a cup of tea cost?)

4. Fourth step — success! I found it!

(jihr-dow) *(shwoh)*
Once **nǐ zhīdào** what **nǐ** would like, **nǐ shuō,**
say

(juh)
Wǒ xiǎng yào zhè ge. _____
this

or simply,

(yow)
Wǒ yào. _____
want

Huòzhě, if **nǐ** don't want something, **nǐ shuō,**

(boo) *(ssee-hoo-ahn)*
Wǒ bù xǐhuān nà ge. _____
don't like

or

Wǒ bù yào. _____

Congratulations! You have finished. By now you should have stuck your labels, flashed your cards, cut out your menu guide and packed your suitcases. You should be very pleased with your accomplishment. You have learned what it sometimes takes others years to achieve and you hopefully had fun doing it. **Yí lù píng ān!** *(ahn)*
safe and peaceful journey

Glossary

This glossary contains words used in this book only. It is not meant to be a dictionary. Consider purchasing a dictionary which best suits your needs - small for traveling, large for reference, or specialized for specific vocabulary needs.

A

ǎi *(I)* .... short
Áodàlìyá *(ow-dah-lee-yah)* .... Australia
Āodìlì *(ow-dee-lee)* .... Austria
āsīpīlín *(ah-sih-pee-leen)* .... aspirin

B

bā *(bah)* .... eight, scar
bá *(bah)* .... to pull up
bǎ *(bah)* .... measure word (M)
bà *(bah)* .... father
bābǎi *(bah-by)* .... eight hundred
bái *(by)* .... white
bǎi *(by)* .... (hundred) combined with other numbers
báicài *(by-tsi)* .... cabbage
bǎihuò diàn *(by-hwoh)(dee-ahn)* .... department store
bàn *(bahn)* .... half, half past
bàngōngshì *(bahn-gohng-shr)* .... office
bāoguǒ *(bao-gwoh)* .... parcel
bǎoshí *(bao-shr)* .... gem
bàozhǐ *(bao-jihr)* .... newspaper
bāshí *(bah-shr)* .... eighty
bāyuè *(bah-yoo-eh)* .... August
bēi *(bay)* .... glass, cup (M)
běi *(bay)* .... north
běibiān *(bay-bee-ahn)* .... North
běifāng *(bay-fahng)* .... northern
bēizi *(bay-zuh)* .... cup, mug
bèizi *(bay-zuh)* .... quilt
běn *(buhn)* .... bound together (M)
běndì cháhàotái *(buhn-dee)(chah-how-tie)* ....
.... local directory assistance
běndì diànhuà *(buhn-dee)(dee-ahn-hwah)* ... local telephone call
bǐ *(bee)* .... pen, writing instrument
biān *(bee-ahn)* .... side
biǎogé *(bee-ow-guh)* .... form, schedule
bǐjī *(bee-jee)* .... handwriting
bǐjì *(bee-jee)* .... to take notes
bǐjìběn *(bee-jee-buhn)* .... notebook
Bǐlìshí *(bee-lee-shr)* .... Belgium
bīng *(beeng)* .... ice
bìng *(beeng)* .... sick
bīngbáo *(beeng-bao)* .... hail
bīnggùn *(beeng-goon)* .... popsicle
bīngkuài *(beeng-kwhy)* .... ice cubes
bīngqílín *(beeng-chee-leen)* .... ice cream
bīngshān *(beeng-shahn)* .... iceberg
bīngshuāng *(beeng-shwahng)* .... frost
bīngtáng *(beeng-tahng)* .... rock candy
bīnguǎn *(been-gwahn)* ...... hotel for foreign tourists
bīngxiāng *(beeng-ssee-ahng)* .... refrigerator
bīngxié *(beeng-ssee-eh)* .... ice skates
bīngzhù *(beeng-joo)* .... icicle
bǐxīn *(bee-sseen)* .... pen/pencil refill
bōcài *(bwoh-tsi)* .... spinach
bōlí *(bwoh-lee)* .... glassware
bōlíbēi *(bwoh-lee-bay)* .... glass
bówùguǎn *(bwoh-woo-gwahn)* .... museum

bù, bú *(boo)* .... no, not
bù hǎo *(boo)(how)* .... not good, bad
bù néng jìnqù *(boo)(nung)(jeen-chee-oo)* ...... do not enter
bú shìhé *(boo)(shr-huh)* .... it does not fit
bú xiè *(boo)(ssee-eh)* .... you're welcome
bú yào *(boo)(yow)* .... don't want it
bùxié *(boo-ssee-eh)* .... cotton shoes

C

cài *(tsi)* .... vegetables, food dishes
càichǎng *(tsi-chahng)* .... market
càidān *(tsi-dahn)* .... menu
càidiàn *(tsi-dee-ahn)* .... vegetable store
càihuā *(tsi-hwah)* .... cauliflower
càiyuán *(tsi-yoo-ahn)* .... vegetable garden
càiyóu *(tsi-yoh)* .... vegetable oil
càizǐr *(tsi-zur)* .... vegetable seeds
cānchē *(tsahn-chuh)* .... dining car
cānjīn *(tsahn-jeen)* .... napkin
cǎo *(tsow)* .... grass
cèsuǒ *(tsuh-swoh)* .... lavatory
chá *(chah)* .... tea
chábēi *(chah-bay)* .... tea cup
chàbùduō *(chah-boo-dwoh)* .... about
chádiǎn *(chah-dee-ahn)* .... light meal
cháguǎn *(chah-gwahn)* .... teahouse
cháhuā *(chah-hwah)* .... camelia
cháhuì *(chah-hway)* .... tea party
chájī *(chah-jee)* .... coffee table
chájù *(chah-joo)* .... tea service
cháng *(chahng)* .... long
chángcháng *(chahng-chahng)* ...... often, generally
Chángchéng *(chahng-chuhng)* .... the Great Wall
chángtú cháhàotái *(chahng-too)(chah-how-tie)* ....
.... long-distance directory assistance
chángtú diànhuà *(chahng-too)(dee-ahn-hwah)* ....
.... long-distance telephone call
chángyǐ *(chahng-yee)* .... bench
chāntīng *(chahn-teeng)* .... hotel café
chǎo *(chow)* .... stir-fried
cháshuǐ *(chah-shway)* .... drink (tea, etc.)
cháyè *(chah-yeh)* .... tea leaf
chāzi *(chah-zuh)* .... fork
chē *(chuh)* .... vehicle, car, cart
chēkù *(chuh-koo)* .... garage
chènqún *(chuhn-choon)* .... underslip
chènyī *(chuhn-yee)* .... shirt, blouse
chēpái *(chuh-pie)* .... license plate
chēxiāng *(chuh-ssee-ahng)* .... compartment
chēzhàn *(chuh-jahn)* .... bus/vehicle stop
chī *(chr)* .... to eat, eats, eat
chǐcùn *(chee-tsoon)* .... measurement, size
chīfàn *(chr-fahn)* .... let's eat, to eat a meal
chuán *(chwahn)* .... boat
chuáng *(chwahng)* .... bed
chuānghù *(chwahng-hoo)* .... window
chuánzhēn *(chwahn-juhn)* .... fax
chúfáng *(choo-fahng)* .... kitchen
chúhànjì *(choo-hahn-jee)* .... deodorant

chūkǒu (choo-koh). . . . . exit
chūnjié (choon-jee-eh). . . . . Chinese New Year
chūnjuǎn (choon-joo-ahn). . . . . spring roll
chūntiān (choon-tee-ahn). . . . . .spring
chūzūchē (choo-zoo-chuh). . . . . taxi
cí (tsih). . . . . word
cídiǎn (tsih-dee-ahn). . . . . dictionary
cóng (tswong) . . . . from

D

dǎ (dah) . . . . to make (telephone call, telegram)
dà (dah) . . . . big, size
dàdào (dah-dow) . . . . boulevard
dài (die) . . . . to bring
dài (die) . . . . with
dàn (dahn). . . . . egg
dānchéng (dahn-chuhng). . . . . one-way
Dānmài (dahn-my) . . . . Denmark
dānrénfáng (dahn-ruhn-fahng) . . . . single room
dào (dow). to, to arrive, arrival
dāozi (dow-zuh) . . . . knife
dàyī (dah-yee). . . . . overcoat
de (duh) . . . . .added to word when an adjective
Déguó (duh-gwoh) . . . . Germany
dēng (dung). . . . . lamp, light
děng (dung). . . . . class of travel
děng (dung). to wait, waits, wait
Déwén (duh-wuhn) . . . . German
dī (dee) . . . . low
diǎn (dee-ahn) . . . . o'clock
diàn (dee-ahn) . . . . .store, shop
diàn (dee-ahn) . . . . electricity
diànchē (dee-ahn-chuh) . . . . trolley
diànchē zhàn (dee-ahn-chuh)(jahn). . . . . trolley stop
diànchí (dee-ahn-chee) . . . . battery
diànhuà (dee-ahn-hwah) . . . . .telephone, telephone call
diànhuà bù (dee-ahn-hwah)(boo) . . . telephone book/register
diànhuà kǎ (dee-ahn-hwah)(kah). . . . . telephone card
diànhuà tíng (dee-ahn-hwah)(teeng) . . . . telephone booth
diànnǎo (dee-ahn-now). . . . . computer
diànqì (dee-ahn-chee) . . . . electronics
diànqì diàn (dee-ahn-chee)(dee-ahn) . . . . electronics store
diànshì (dee-ahn-shr) . . . . television
diàntái (dee-ahn-tie) . . . . radio station
diàntī (dee-ahn-tee) . . . . elevator
diàntǒng (dee-ahn-twong) . . . . flashlight
diǎnxīn (dee-ahn-sseen). . . . . snack
diǎnxíngde (dee-ahn-sseeng-duh). . . . . typical
diànyǐng (dee-ahn-yeeng). . . . . movie
diànyǐngyuàn (dee-ahn-yeeng-yoo-ahn) . . . . . movie theater
diànyuán (dee-ahn-yoo-ahn). . . . . store clerk
diànzhǔ (dee-ahn-joo). storekeeper
diànzi yóujiàn (dee-ahn-zih)(yoh-jee-ahn) . . . . email
diāokè (dee-ow-kuh) . . . . carvings
dìbā (dee-bah) . . . . eighth
dìbǎn (dee-bahn) . . . . floor
dìfāng (dee-fahng) . . . . place
dìng (deeng) . . . . to book, reserve
dìngdān (deeng-dahn). .order form
dìqī (dee-chee) . . . . seventh
dìtú (dee-too). . . . . map
diū (dee-oo) . . . . .to lose
dìxiàshì (dee-ssee-ah-shr) . . . . basement
dìtiě (dee-tee-eh) . . . . .subway
dìtiě zhàn (dee-tee-eh)(jahn) . . . . subway stop
dōng (dwong). . . . . .east
dǒng (dwong) . . . . . . to understand, understands, understand

dōngbiān (dwong-bee-ahn). . . . . East
dòngcí (dwong-tsih). . . . . verb
dōngfāng (dwong-fahng) . . . . eastern, oriental
dōngnán (dwong-nahn) . . . . east-south
dōngtiān (dwong-tee-ahn) . . . . winter
dòngwùyuán (dwong-woo-yoo-ahn) . . . . zoo
dōngxi (dwong-ssee) . . . . .thing
dōu (doh) . . . . all
dòu (doh) . . . . bean
dòufu (doh-foo). . . . . bean curd
dòushā (doh-shah) . . . . bean paste
dòuyá (doh-yah) . . . . bean sprouts
dòuyóu (doh-yoh) . . . . soybean oil
dù (doo) . . . . degrees
duǎn (dwahn) . . . . .short
duǎnkù (dwahn-koo). . . . . .shorts
duìbùqǐ (dway-boo-chee). . . . . I'm sorry, excuse me
duìhuà (dway-hwah). . . . . conversation
duìhuàn chù (dway-hwahn)(choo) . . . money-exchange office
duō (dwoh) . . . . .many, much, more, a lot
duōshao (dwoh-shao) . . . . how much, how many
duōshao qián (dwoh-shao)(chee-ahn) . . . .
. . . . .how much does that cost, how much money

E

é (uh) . . . . goose
èr (ur). . . . . two, second
èrbǎi (ur-by) . . . . two hundred
èrshí (ur-shr) . . . . twenty
èryuè (ur-yoo-eh) . . . . February
érzi (ur-zuh) . . . . son

F

fā piào (fah)(pee-ow) . . . . bill
Fǎguó (fah-gwoh) . . . . France
fàn (fahn) . . . . .meal, rice
fàndiàn (fahn-dee-ahn). . . . . tourist hotel
fāng (fahng) . . . . direction
fáng (fahng) . . . . room, apartment
fángdōng (fahng-dwong) . . . . landlord
fāngfǎ (fahng-fah) . . . . .ways
fángjiān (fahng-jee-ahn) . . . . .room
fángkè (fahng-kuh) . . . . .tenant
fànguǎn (fahn-gwahn) . . . . restaurant
fángzi (fahng-zuh) . . . . house
fángzide (fahng-zuh-duh). . . . . .house's
fàntīng (fahn-teeng) . . . . .dining room
Fǎwén (fah-wuhn) . . . . French
fēi (fay). . . . . to fly, flies, fly
fēijī (fay-jee) . . . . airplane
fēijīchǎng (fay-jee-chahng) . . . . airport
fēijīkù (fay-jee-koo). . . . . hangar (airport)
fēijīpiào (fay-jee-pee-ow) . . . . .airplane ticket
fēiqín (fay-cheen). . . . . .birds
fēisù (fay-soo). . . . . quickly
fēiwǔ (fay-woo) . . . . to flutter
fēixíng (fay-sseeng). . . . . to soar
fēixíngyuán (fay-sseeng-yoo-ahn) . . . . pilot
fēiyú (fay-yoo) . . . . .flying fish
féizào (fay-zow) . . . . soap
fēn (fuhn) . . . . .minute, unit of Chinese money
fěnbǐ (fuhn-bee) . . . . .chalk
fēng (fung) . . . . measure word (M)
fēngqín (fung-cheen). . . . . organ
fěnhóng (fuhn-hohng). . . . . pink
fójiào (fwoh-jee-ow) . . . . Buddhist
fù qián (foo)(chee-ahn) . . . . .to pay, pay for **109**

fùmǔ *(foo-moo)* . . . . parents
fùqin *(foo-cheen)* . . . . father
fúwùyuán *(foo-woo-yoo-ahn)* . . . . service person

G

gānbēi *(gahn-bay)* . . . . cheers!
gāngbǐ *(gahng-bee)* . . . . fountain pen
gāngqín *(gahng-cheen)* . . . . piano
gānxǐ diàn *(gahn-ssee)(dee-ahn)* . . . . dry cleaners
gāo *(gao)* . . . . high, tall
ge *(guh)* . . . . measure word (M)
gēge *(guh-guh)* . . . . (older) brother
géi *(gay)* . . . . for
gěi *(gay)* . . . . to give, give, gives
gěi wǒ *(gay)(woh)* . . . . give me
gēzi *(guh-zuh)* . . . . pigeon
gōnggòngqìchē *(gohng-gohng-chee-chuh)* . . . . bus
gōnggòngqìchē zhàn *(gohng-gohng-chee-chuh)(jahn)* . . . . . .
. . . . bus stop
gōngjù *(gohng-joo)* . . . . tools
gōngyìpǐn *(gohng-yee-peen)* . . . . artworks
gōngyòng diànhuà *(gohng-yohng)(dee-ahn-hwah)* . . . .
. . . . public telephone
gōngyù *(gohng-yoo)* . . . . apartment, boarding room
gōngyuán *(gohng-yoo-ahn)* . . . . park
gǒu *(goh)* . . . . dog
guāfēng *(gwah-fung)* . . . . windy
guāliǎndāo *(gwah-lee-ahn-dow)* . . . . .razor
guǎn *(gwahn)* . . . . place, hall
guān *(gwahn)* . . . . closes
guānmén *(gwahn-muhn)* . . . . .closed, closes
gǔdǒng diàn *(goo-dwong)(dee-ahn)* . . . . .antique store
gūgu *(goo-goo)* . . . . aunt
guì *(gway)* . . . . .expensive
guìtái *(gway-tie)* . . . . counter
guìzi *(gway-zuh)* . . . . cupboard
gùkè fúwù *(goo-kuh)(foo-woo)* . . . . . . customer service
guó *(gwoh)* . . . . country, nation, state
guógē *(gwoh-guh)* . . . . national anthem
guóhuì *(gwoh-hway)* . . . . .parliament
guójí *(gwoh-jee)* . . . . nationality
guójiā *(gwoh-jee-ah)* . . . . country
guómín *(gwoh-meen)* . . . . people of a country
guónèi *(gwoh-nay)* . . . . domestic
guóqí *(gwoh-chee)* . . . . national flag
guóqìng jié *(gwoh-cheeng)(jee-eh)* . .National Day (October 1)
guówài *(gwoh-why)* . . . . international
guówáng *(gwoh-wahng)* . . . . king
guóyíng *(gwoh-yeeng)* .state-owned

H

hái *(hi)* . . . . still
hǎi *(hi)* . . . . sea
hǎi àn *(hi)(ahn)* . . . . .coast
hǎi lán bǎoshí *(hi)(lahn)(bao-shr)* . . . . .aquamarine
hǎigǎng *(hi-gahng)* . . . . .seaport, harbor
hǎiguān *(hi-gwahn)* . . . . customs
hǎimián *(hi-mee-ahn)* . . . . sponge
háishì *(hi-shr)* . . . . or
hǎitān *(hi-tahn)* . . . . beach
hǎiwài *(hi-why)* . . . . .overseas
hǎiwān *(hi-wahn)* . . . . bay, gulf
hǎiwèi *(hi-way)* . . . . .seafood
hǎixiān *(hi-ssee-ahn)* . . . . .seafood
hǎiyáng *(hi-yahng)* . . . . ocean
hángkōngxìn *(hahng-kwong-sseen)* . . . . airmail
110 hǎo *(how)* . . . . .good, well, okay, all right

hào *(how)* . . . . number
hǎochī *(how-chr)* . . . . .delicious
hǎochù *(how-choo)* . . . . benefit
hǎogǎn *(how-gahn)* . . . . good impression
hǎohàn *(how-hahn)* . . . . wise man, hero
hǎokàn *(how-kahn)* . . . . good-looking
hǎotīng *(how-teeng)* . . . . pleasant to the ear
hǎoxiào *(how-ssee-ow)* . . . . funny
hǎoyì *(how-yee)* . . . . .goodwill
hǎoyùn *(how-yoon)* . . . . good fortune
hē *(huh)* . . . . to drink, drinks, drink
hé *(huh)* . . . . and
hēi *(hay)* . . . . .black
Hélán *(huh-lahn)* . . . . Netherlands
hěn *(huhn)* . . . . very
hóng *(hohng)* . . . . red
hóng bǎoshí *(hohng)(bao-shr)* . . . . ruby
hòubiān *(hoh-bee-ahn)* . . . . behind
hòuchēshì *(hoh-chuh-shr)* . . . . .waiting room
huā *(hwah)* . . . . flower, multi-colored
huà *(hwah)* . . . . language
huā duǒ *(hwah)(dwoh)* . . . . blossom
huài *(hwhy)* . . . . bad
huàn chē *(hwahn)(chuh)* . . . . to transfer (vehicles)
huáng *(hwahng)* . . . . .yellow
huā píng *(hwah)(peeng)* . . . . flower vase
huā quān *(hwah)(chwahn)* . . . . wreath
huā shù *(hwah)(shoo)* . . . . bouquet
huār *(hwahr)* . . . . .flower
huār diàn *(hwahr)(dee-ahn)* . . . . flower shop
huàr *(hwahr)* . . . . picture
huáshì *(hwah-shr)* . . . . Fahrenheit
huāyuán *(hwah-yoo-ahn)* . . . . garden
huī *(hway)* . . . . gray
huíjiào *(hway-jee-ow)* . . . . Moslem
hújiāo *(hoo-jee-ow)* . . . . pepper
huǒ *(hwoh)* . . . . fire, flame
huǒchái *(hwoh-chi)* . . . . .match
huǒchē *(hwoh-chuh)* . . . . train
huǒchē zhàn *(hwoh-chuh)(jahn)* . . . . train station
huǒchē zǒng zhàn *(hwoh-chuh)(zwong)(jahn)* . . . .
. . . . .main train station
huǒjiàn *(hwoh-jee-ahn)* . . . . .rocket
huǒshān *(hwoh-shahn)* . . . . .volcano
huòzhě *(hwoh-juh)* . . . . or
hùzhào *(hoo-jow)* . . . . .passport

J

jī *(jee)* . . . . .chicken
jǐ *(jee)* . . . . some, several
jǐ *(jee)* . . . . how many
jì *(jee)* . . . . to send by mail, mail
jǐ diǎn le? *(jee)(dee-ahn)(luh)* . . . . what time is it?
jiā *(jee-ah)* . . . . home
jiāhuǒ *(jee-ah-hwoh)* . . . . .(that) thing, guy, weapon
jiājù *(jee-ah-joo)* . . . . furniture
jiān *(jee-ahn)* . . . . measure word (M)
Jiānádà *(jee-ah-nah-dah)* . . . . .Canada
Jiānádà rén *(jee-ah-nah-dah)(ruhn)* . . . . Canadian
jiàngluò *(jee-ahng-lwoh)* . . . . to land
jiànkāng *(jee-ahn-kahng)* . . . . .healthy
jiànkāng zhèngmíng shū *(jee-ahn-kahng)(jung-meeng)*
(shoo) . . . . health certificate
jiǎo *(jee-ow)* . . . . .unit of Chinese money
jiào *(jee-ow)* . . . . to be called, named
jiào *(jee-ow)* . . . . .to ask, yell, call for
jiào *(jee-ow)* . . . . to order, orders, order
jiāojuǎn *(jee-ow-joo-ahn)* . . . . .film

jiàqián (jee-ah-chee-ahn) . . . . prices
jiārén (jee-ah-ruhn) . . . . family members
jiātíng (jee-ah-teeng) . . . . family
jiāyóu zhàn (jee-ah-yoh)(jahn) . . . . service station
jīdàn (jee-dahn) . . . . chicken eggs
jīdūjiào (jee-doo-jee-ow) . . . . Protestant
jiē (jee-eh) . . . . street
jié (jee-eh) . . . . to clear, pay, close
jiézhàng (jee-eh-jahng) . . . . to pay a bill
jīn (jeen) . . . . golden
jìn (jeen) . . . . into, in
jīn nián (jeen)(nee-ahn) . . . . this year
jìn zhǐ tōng xíng (jeen)(jihr)(twong)(sseng) . . no trespassing
jìn zhǐ zhàoxiàng (jeen)(jihr)(jow-ssee-ahng) . . . .
. . . . no photos allowed
jǐngchá (jeeng-chah) . . . . police
jīnglǐ (jeeng-lee) . . . . manager
jìngzi (jeeng-zuh) . . . . mirror
jìniànpǐn (jee-nee-ahn-peen) . . . . souvenirs
jìniànpǐn diàn (jee-nee-ahn-peen)(dee-ahn) . . . souvenir store
jīntiān (jeen-tee-ahn) . . . . today
jīpiào (jee-pee-ow) . . . . flight
jípǔchē (jee-poo-chuh) . . . . jeep
jiǔ (jee-oo) . . . . wine
jiǔ (jee-oo) . . . . nine
jiǔ guǎn (jee-oo)(gwahn) . . . . tavern
jiǔbǎi (jee-oo-by) . . . . nine hundred
jiǔbēi (jee-oo-bay) . . . . wine glass
jiǔdiàn (jee-oo-dee-ahn) . . . . . . hotel for foreign tourists
jiùmìng (jee-oo-meeng) . . . . help!
jiǔshí (jee-oo-shr) . . . . ninety
jiǔyuè (jee-oo-yoo-eh) . . . . September
jīyā (jee-yah) . . . . poultry
júhóngsè (joo-hohng-suh) . . . . orange
júhuā (joo-hwah) . . . . chrysanthemum
jùyuàn (joo-yoo-ahn) . . . . theater
júzishuǐ (joo-zuh-shway) . . . . orange juice

K

kāfēi (kah-fay) . . . . coffee
kāfēi guǎn (kah-fay)(gwahn) . . . . coffee shop
kāfēisè (kah-fay-suh) . . . . brown (coffee-colored)
kāi (ki) . . . . to open, open, opens
kāi (ki) . . . . to leave, depart, departure
kàn (kahn) . . . . to read (books), look at
kànjiàn (kahn-jee-ahn) . . . . to see, sees, see
kǎo (kow) . . . . broiled, baked
kètīng (kuh-teeng) . . . . living room
kǒuqín (koh-cheen) . . . . harmonica
kuài (kwhy) . . . . fast, unit of Chinese money
kuàichē (kwhy-chuh) . . . . fast train
kuàizi (kwhy-zuh) . . . . chopsticks
kuàngquán shuǐ (kwahng-choo-ahn)(shway) . . mineral water
kùwà (koo-wah) . . . . pantyhose
kùzi (koo-zuh) . . . . trousers

L

lā (lah) . . . . to pull
là (lah) . . . . wax
làbǐ (lah-bee) . . . . crayon
lái (lie) . . . . to come, come, comes
láihuí (lie-hway) . . . . round-trip
lán (lahn) . . . . blue
lán bǎoshí (lahn)(bao-shr) . . . . sapphire
lánhuā (lahn-hwah) . . . . orchid
lǎo (lao) . . . . old
Lǎowō (lao-woh) . . . . Laos

làtái (lah-tie) . . . . candlestick
làzhǐ (lah-jihr) . . . . wax paper
làzhú (lah-joo) . . . . candle
le (luh) . . . . with a verb indicating completed action
lěng (lung) . . . . cold
lěngpán (lung-pahn) . . . . appetizers
lǐ (lee) . . . . inside
liǎng (lee-ahng) . . . . two
liàng (lee-ahng) . . . . measure word (M)
liǎngbǎi (lee-ahng-by) . . . . two hundred
liángxié (lee-ahng-ssee-eh) . . . . sandals
liányīqún (lee-ahn-yee-choon) . . . . dress
lièjiǔ (lee-eh-jee-oo) . . . . spirits (alcohol)
lǐfà diàn (lee-fah)(dee-ahn) . . . . hairdressers
lǐfàguǎn (lee-fah-gwahn) . . . . barber shop
líng (leeng) . . . . zero
lǐngdài (leeng-die) . . . . tie
língqián (leeng-chee-ahn) . . . . change (money)
línyù (leen-yoo) . . . . shower
lìshǐ (lee-shr) . . . . history
liù (lee-oo) . . . . six
liùbǎi (lee-oo-by) . . . . six hundred
liùshí (lee-oo-shr) . . . . sixty
liùyī értóng jié (lee-oo-yee)(ur-tohng)(jee-eh) . . . .
. . . . Children's Day (June 1)
liùyuè (lee-oo-yoo-eh) . . . . June
lóu (loh) . . . . floor
lù (loo) . . . . road, route
lǜ (loo) . . . . green
lǚguǎn (loo-gwahn) . . . . hotel
lǚguǎn de chāntīng (loo-gwahn)(duh)(chahn-teeng) . . . .
. . . . hotel café
lǚguǎn jīnglǐ (loo-gwahn)(jeeng-lee) . . . . hotel manager
lǚkè (loo-kuh) . . . . passenger, traveler, tourist
lǜsè (loo-suh) . . . . green-colored
lǚxíng (loo-sseng) . . . . to travel, travels, travel
lǚxíng shè (loo-sseng)(shuh) . . . . travel agent, travel agency
lǚxíng zhīpiào (loo-sseng)(jihr-pee-ow) . . . traveler's checks
lúzi (loo-zuh) . . . . stove

M

ma (mah) . . . . used at end of yes-no questions
mā (mah) . . . . mother
má (mah) . . . . hemp
mǎ (mah) . . . . horse
mà (mah) . . . . curse
mǎi (my) . . . . to buy, buys, buy
mài (my) . . . . to sell, sells, sell
mǎmǎhūhū (mah-mah-hoo-hoo) . . . . so-so
màn (mahn) . . . . slow
màn man (mahn)(mahn) . . . . slowly
māo (mao) . . . . cat
máo (mao) . . . . wool, unit of Chinese money
máobǐ (mao-bee) . . . . writing brush
máojīn (mao-jeen) . . . . towel
máopí (mao-pee) . . . . fur
máoyī (mao-yee) . . . . sweater
màozi (mao-zuh) . . . . hat
máquè (mah-choo-eh) . . . . sparrow
mǎtǒng (mah-twong) . . . . toilet
méi (may) . . . . coal
méi yǒu (may)(yoh) . . . . have not had
méiguìhuā (may-gway-hwah) . . . . rose
Měiguó (may-gwoh) . . . . the United States
méikuàng (may-kwahng) . . . . coal mine
mèimei (may-may) . . . . (younger) sister
méiqì (may-chee) . . . . gas

méiqìlú *(may-chee-loo)* . . . . gas stove
měishùguǎn *(may-shoo-gwahn)* . . . . art gallery
méiyóu *(may-yoh)* . . . . kerosene
mén *(muhn)* . . . . door, gate
Měnggǔ *(muhng-goo)* . . . . Mongolia
mǐ *(mee)* . . . . rice
mì *(mee)* . . . . honey
miàn *(mee-ahn)* . . . . noodles
miàn fàn *(mee-ahn)(fahn)* . . . . noodles and rice dishes
miàn guǎn *(mee-ahn)(gwahn)* . . . . noodle shop
miànbāo *(mee-ahn-bao)* . . . . bread
miànbāo diàn *(mee-ahn-bao)(dee-ahn)* . . . . bakery
miànbāochē *(mee-ahn-bao-chuh)* . . . . van
miǎo *(mee-ow)* . . . . second
miào *(mee-ow)* . . . . temple
mǐfàn *(mee-fahn)* . . . . cooked rice
mǐfěn *(mee-fuhn)* . . . . rice noodle
mìfēng *(mee-fung)* . . . . honeybee
mìjiàn *(mee-jee-ahn)* . . . . candied fruit
mǐjiǔ *(mee-jee-oo)* . . . . rice wine
mìjú *(mee-joo)* . . . . tangerine
míng nián *(meeng)(nee-ahn)* . . . . next year
míngtiān *(meeng-tee-ahn)* . . . . tomorrow
míngtiān jiàn *(meeng-tee-ahn)(jee-ahn)* . . . see you tomorrow
míngxìnpiàn *(meeng-sseen-pee-ahn)* . . . . postcard
míngzì *(meeng-zih)* . . . . name
mǐsè *(mee-suh)* . . . . cream-colored
mìyuè *(mee-yoo-eh)* . . . . honeymoon
mǔqin *(moo-cheen)* . . . . mother

N

nǎ *(nah)* . . . . where, which
nà *(nah)* . . . . that, those
nán *(nahn)* . . . . male
nán *(nahn)* . . . . south
nánbiān *(nahn-bee-ahn)* . . . . South
nánfāng *(nahn-fahng)* . . . . southern
Nánfēi *(nahn-fay)* . . . . South Africa
nánrén *(nahn-ruhn)* . . . . man, men
nánzhuāng *(nahn-jwahng)* . . . . men's clothing
nàozhōng *(now-jwong)* . . . . alarm clock
nǎr *(nahr)* . . . . where
náshǒucài *(nah-shoh-tsi)* . . . . specialties (food)
něi *(nay)* . . . . which
nèikù *(nay-koo)* . . . . underpants
nèiyī *(nay-yee)* . . . . undershirt
néng *(nung)* . . . . to be able to, can
nǐ *(nee)* . . . . you
Nǐ hǎo ma? *(nee)(how)(mah)* . . . . How are you?
Nǐ jiào shénme míngzì? *(nee)(jee-ow)(shun-muh)*
   (meeng-zih) . . . . . How are you called?, What is your name?
nián *(nee-ahn)* . . . . year
niánqīng *(nee-ahn-cheeng)* . . . . young
niǎo *(nee-ow)* . . . . bird
niǎolóng *(nee-ow-lwong)* . . . . birdcage
nǐde *(nee-duh)* . . . . your
nǐmen *(nee-muhn)* . . . . you (as in you all, you guys)
nín zǎo *(neen)(zow)* . . . . good morning
nínhǎo *(neen-how)* . . . . hello
niú *(nee-oo)* . . . . cow
niúdú *(nee-oo-doo)* . . . . calf
niújiǎo *(nee-oo-jee-ow)* . . . . horn
niúnǎi *(nee-oo-ni)* . . . . milk
niúnǎi diàn *(nee-oo-ni)(dee-ahn)* . . . . dairy
niúpái *(nee-oo-pie)* . . . . beefsteak
niúpí *(nee-oo-pee)* . . . . leather
112 niúpí zhǐ *(nee-oo-pee)(jihr)* . . . . brown paper

niúròu *(nee-oo-roh)* . . . . beef
niúwěi *(nee-oo-way)* . . . . oxtail
niúyóu *(nee-oo-yoh)* . . . . butter
niúzǎikù *(nee-oo-zi-koo)* . . . . jeans
nǔ *(noo)* . . . . female
nuǎnhuo *(noo-ahn-hwoh)* . . . . warm
nǚér *(noo-ur)* . . . . daughter
Nuówēi *(nwoh-way)* . . . . Norway
nǚrén *(noo-ruhn)* . . . . woman, women
nǚzhuāng *(noo-jwahng)* . . . . women's clothing

O

Ōuzhōu *(oh-joh)* . . . . Europe

P

pán *(pahn)* . . . . plate, portion (M)
pángbiān *(pahng-bee-ahn)* . . . . next to
pánzi *(pahn-zuh)* . . . . plate
péngyou *(pung-yoh)* . . . . friend
piányí *(pee-ahn-yee)* . . . . inexpensive
piào *(pee-ow)* . . . . ticket
píbāo *(pee-bao)* . . . . purse, handbag
píjiāzi *(pee-jee-ah-zuh)* . . . . wallet
píjiǔ *(pee-jee-oo)* . . . . beer
píng *(peeng)* . . . . bottle
píngguǒ *(peeng-gwoh)* . . . . apple
píngguǒyuán *(peeng-gwoh-yoo-ahn)* . . . . apple orchard
pízhì pǐn *(pee-jihr)(peen)* . . . . leather
pǔtōngchē *(poo-tohng-chuh)* . . . . ordinary train
pǔtōnghuà *(poo-tohng-hwah)* . . . . common language

Q

qī *(chee)* . . . . seven
qí *(chee)* . . . . to ride
qián *(chee-ahn)* . . . . money
qiānbǐ *(chee-ahn-bee)* . . . . pencil
qiánbiān *(chee-ahn-bee-ahn)* . . . . in front of
qiángjiǎo *(chee-ahng-jee-ow)* . . . . corner
qiānzhèng *(chee-ahn-jung)* . . . . visa
qībǎi *(chee-by)* . . . . seven hundred
qìchē *(chee-chuh)* . . . . car
qiè wù rùnèi *(chee-eh)(woo)(roo-nay)* . . . . keep out
qín *(cheen)* . . . . musical instrument
qíncài *(cheen-tsi)* . . . . celery
qǐng *(cheeng)* . . . . please
qīngcài *(cheeng-tsi)* . . . . green vegetables
qǐngwèn *(cheeng-wuhn)* . . . . excuse me, may I ask
qióng *(chee-oong)* . . . . poor
qīshí *(chee-shr)* . . . . seventy
qiūtiān *(chee-yoo-tee-ahn)* . . . . autumn
qiúxié *(chee-yoo-ssee-eh)* . . . . sport shoes
qìwēn *(chee-wuhn)* . . . . temperature
qīyuè *(chee-yoo-eh)* . . . . July
qù *(choo)* . . . . to go (to, into), go, goes
qù nián *(choo)(nee-ahn)* . . . . last year
qúnzi *(choon-zuh)* . . . . skirt

R

rè *(ruh)* . . . . hot
rén *(ruhn)* . . . . person
rénkǒu *(ruhn-koh)* . . . . population
rénlèi *(ruhn-lay)* . . . . mankind
rénlì *(ruhn-lee)* . . . . manpower
rénmen *(ruhn-muhn)* . . . . people
rénqún *(ruhn-choon)* . . . . crowd
rénxíngdào *(ruhn-ssseng-dow)* . . . . sidewalk
rénzào *(ruhn-zow)* . . . . man-made

rénzhǒng *(ruhn-jwong)* . . . . human race
Rìběn *(ree-buhn)* . . . . Japan
rìlì *(rur-lee)* . . . . calendar
Rìwén *(ree-wuhn)* . . . . Japanese
róngyì *(rohng-yee)* . . . . easy
ròu *(roh)* . . . . meat
ròu diàn *(roh)(dee-ahn)* . . . . butcher shop
rùkǒu *(roo-koh)* . . . . entrance

S

sān *(sahn)* . . . . three
sǎn *(sahn)* . . . . umbrella
sān nián *(sahn)(nee-ahn)* . . . . three years
sānbǎi *(sahn-by)* . . . . three hundred
sānlúnchē *(sahn-loon-chuh)* . . . . pedicab
sānshí *(sahn-shr)* . . . . thirty
sānyuè *(sahn-yoo-eh)* . . . . March
sèlā *(suh-lah)* . . . . salad
shāfā *(shah-fah)* . . . . sofa
shàng *(shahng)* . . . . up, on, on top of
shàngbiān *(shahng-bee-ahn)* . . . . over, above
shāngdiàn *(shahng-dee-ahn)* . . . . store
shàngwǔ *(shahng-woo)* . . . . morning
shàngyī *(shahng-yee)* . . . . jacket, upper outer garment
shāo *(shao)* . . . . roasted
shǎo *(shao)* . . . . little, few
shéi *(shay)* . . . . who
shēngcài *(shuhng-tsi)* . . . . lettuce
shénme *(shun-muh)* . . . . what
shénme dìfāng *(shun-muh)(dee-fahng)* . . . what place, where
shénme rén *(shun-muh)(ruhn)* . . . . what person, who
shénme shíhou *(shun-muh)(shr-hoh)* . . . . . when, what time
shèshì *(shuh-shr)* . . . . Centigrade
shí *(shr)* . . . . stone, rock
shí *(shr)* . . . . ten
shì *(shr)* . . . . to be, am, is, are
shì *(shr)* . . . . yes
shíbā *(shr-bah)* . . . . eighteen
shídiāo *(shr-dee-ow)* . . . . carved stone
shíèr *(shr-ur)* . . . . twelve
shíèryuè *(shr-ur-yoo-eh)* . . . . December
shìhé *(shr-huh)* . . . . it fits
shíjiān *(shr-jee-ahn)* . . . . time
shíjiān biǎo *(shr-jee-ahn)(bee-ow)* . . . . hours, time schedule
shíjiǔ *(shr-jee-oo)* . . . . nineteen
shíkuài *(shr-kwhy)* . . . . boulder
shíliù *(shr-lee-oo)* . . . . sixteen
shímò *(shr-mwoh)* . . . . graphite
shípǐn diàn *(shr-peen)(dee-ahn)* . . . . grocery store
shípǔ *(shr-poo)* . . . . cookbook, recipes
shíqī *(shr-chee)* . . . . seventeen
shísān *(shr-sahn)* . . . . thirteen
shísì *(shr-sih)* . . . . fourteen
shísù *(shr-soo)* . . . . room and board
shíwǔ *(shr-woo)* . . . . fifteen
shíwù *(shr-woo)* . . . . food
shíwǔ fēn *(shr-woo)(fuhn)* . . fifteen minutes, a quarter (time)
shīwù zhāolǐng *(shr-woo)(jow-leeng)* . . . lost-and-found office
shíyī *(shr-yee)* . . . . eleven
shíyīng *(shr-yeeng)* . . . . quartz
shíyīyuè *(shr-yee-yoo-eh)* . . . . November
shíyù *(shr-yoo)* . . . . appetite
shíyuè *(shr-yoo-eh)* . . . . October
shízhǐ *(shr-jihr)* . . . . index finger
shōu *(shoh)* . . . . to take, accept
shōujù *(shoh-joo)* . . . . receipt
shǒujī *(shoh-jee)* . . . . cell phone
shǒujuàn *(shoh-joo-ahn)* . . . . handkerchief

shòupiào chù *(shoh-pee-ow)(choo)* . . . . ticket office
shòupiàoyuán *(shoh-pee-ow-yoo-ahn)* . . ticket seller, conductor
shōushi *(shoh-shr)* . . . . to pack
shǒutào *(shoh-tao)* . . . . gloves
shū *(shoo)* . . . . book
shuāngrénfáng *(shwahng-ruhn-fahng)* . . . . double room
shūbào *(shoo-bao)* . . . . bookbag
shūbào tān *(shoo-bao)(tahn)* . . . . bookstand
shúcài *(shoo-tsi)* . . . . vegetables
shūchú *(shoo-choo)* . . . . bookcase
shūdiàn *(shoo-dee-ahn)* . . . . bookstore
shūfǎ *(shoo-fah)* . . . . handwriting, calligraphy
shūfáng *(shoo-fahng)* . . . . study, den
shūjià *(shoo-jee-ah)* . . . . bookshelf
shuǐ *(shway)* . . . . water
shuì *(shway)* . . . . to sleep
shuì gè hǎo jiào *(shway)(guh)(how)(jee-ow)* . . . . . sleep well!
shuǐbà *(shway-bah)* . . . . dam
shuǐcǎi *(shway-tsi)* . . . . watercolor
shuǐchē *(shway-chuh)* . . . . watermill
shuǐchí *(shway-chr)* . . . . pool
shuìfáng *(shway-fahng)* . . . . bedroom
shuǐfèn *(shway-fuhn)* . . . . moisture
shuǐguǒ *(shway-gwoh)* . . . . fresh fruit
shuǐguǒ diàn *(shway-gwoh)(dee-ahn)* . . . . fruit store
shuǐkù *(shway-koo)* . . . . reservoir
shuǐpáo *(shway-pow)* . . . . bathrobe
shuǐpíng *(shway-peeng)* . . . . water bottle
shuǐshǒu *(shway-shoh)* . . . . sailor
shuìyī *(shway-yee)* . . . . nightshirt, pajamas
shuǐzāi *(shway-zi)* . . . . flood
shuǐzúguǎn *(shway-zoo-gwahn)* . . . . aquarium
shuō *(shwoh)* . . . . to say, speak
shuōhuà *(shwoh-hwah)* . . . . speaking
shūpíng *(shoo-peeng)* . . . . book review
shūqiān *(shoo-chee-ahn)* . . . . bookmark
shúi *(shway)* . . . . who
shúshí diàn *(shoo-shr)(dee-ahn)* . . . . delicatessen
shūshu *(shoo-shoo)* . . . . uncle
shūzhuō *(shoo-jwoh)* . . . . desk
shūzi *(shoo-zuh)* . . . . comb
shùzì *(shoo-zih)* . . . . number
sī *(sih)* . . . . silk
sì *(sih)* . . . . four
sìbǎi *(sih-by)* . . . . four hundred
sìshí *(sih-shr)* . . . . forty
sìyuè *(sih-yoo-eh)* . . . . April

T

tā *(tah)* . . . . he, she, it, him, her
táidēng *(tie-dung)* . . . . table lamp
Tàiguó *(tie-gwoh)* . . . . Thailand
tàipíng mén *(tie-peeng)(muhn)* . . . . emergency gate
tàitài *(tie-tie)* . . . . Mrs.
tàiyáng *(tie-yahng)* . . . . sun
tàiyáng yǎnjìng *(tie-yahng)(yahn-jeeng)* . . . . sunglasses
tāmen *(tah-muhn)* . . . . they, them
tāng *(tahng)* . . . . soup
tāngchí *(tahng-chr)* . . . . soup spoon
tǎngyǐ *(tahng-yee)* . . . . . reclining seats, recliner, reclining car
tāngyuán *(tahng-yoo-ahn)* . . . . sweet rice-flour ball
tèbié *(tuh-bee-uh)* . . . . especially
tī *(tee)* . . . . ladder
tí *(tee)* . . . . to lift
tǐ *(tee)* . . . . body
tì *(tee)* . . . . tears
tiān *(tee-ahn)* . . . . day
tiándiǎn *(tee-ahn-dee-ahn)* . . . . dessert

113

tiānqì *(tee-ahn-chee)* . . . . weather
tiāntiān *(tee-ahn-tee-ahn)* . . . . everyday
tiānwéntái *(tee-ahn-wuhn-tie)* . . . . .observatory
tiānzhǔjiào *(tee-ahn-joo-jee-ow)* . . . . Catholic
tiáo *(tee-ow)* . . . . measure word (M)
tiěguǐ *(tee-eh-gway)* . . . . .track
tīng *(teeng)* . . . . listen to
tíng *(teeng)* . . . . booth
tíngchē chǎng *(teeng-chuh)(chahng)* . . . . .parking lot
tíngliú *(teeng-lee-oo)* . . . . to stay, stays, stay
tīngtǒng *(teeng-tohng)* . . . . receiver
tíqín *(tee-cheen)* . . . . violin
tǐyùguǎn *(tee-yoo-gwahn)* . . . . gymnasium
tóu děng *(toh)(dung)* . . . . first class
tú *(too)* . . . . .disciple
tuī *(tway)* . . . . .to push
tuōxié *(twoh-ssee-eh)* . . . . slippers
túshūguǎn *(too-shoo-gwahn)* . . . . library

W

wàiguó *(why-gwoh)* .foreign
wàitào *(why-tao)* . . . . .jacket
wǎn *(wahn)* . . . . evening, night
wǎn ān *(wahn)(ahn)* . . . . good night
wǎnfàn *(wahn-fahn)* . . . . .dinner, supper
wánjù *(wahn-joo)* . . . . toys
wǎnshàng *(wahn-shahng)* . . . . evening
wǎnshàng jiàn *(wahn-shahng)(jee-ahn)* . . . .see you in the evening
wàzi *(wah-zuh)* . . . . socks
wèi *(way)* . . . . hey, hello
wèishēngzhǐ *(way-shung-jihr)* . . . . toilet paper
wèishénme *(way-shun-muh)* . . . . .why
wén *(wuhn)* . . . . written language
wèn *(wuhn)* . . . . to ask, asks, ask
wénhuàshān *(wuhn-hwah-shahn)* . . . . T-shirt
wénjiàn *(wuhn-jee-ahn)* . . . . .documents
wénjù *(wuhn-joo-we)* . . . . stationery
wénjù diàn *(wuhn-joo)(dee-ahn)* . . . . stationery store
wèntí *(wuhn-tee)* . . . . .question
wǒ *(woh)* . . . . .I, me
wǒ è le *(woh)(uh)(luh)* . . . . I'm hungry
wǒ kǒu kě *(woh)(koh)(kuh)* . . . . .I'm thirsty
wǒ mílù le *(woh)(mee-loo)(luh)* . . . . .I'm lost
wǒ shì *(woh)(shr)* . . . . I am
wǒ zài *(woh)(zi)* . . . . I am (in, at)
wǒde *(woh-duh)* . . . . my
wǒmen *(woh-muhn)* . . . . we, us
wòpù *(woh-poo)* . . . . .sleeping car
wǔ *(woo)* . . . . five
wǔbǎi *(woo-by)* . . . . five hundred
wǔfàn *(woo-fahn)* . . . . .lunch, mid-day meal
wǔqiān *(woo-chee-ahn)* . . . . .five thousand
wǔshí *(woo-shr)* . . . . .fifty
wūyā *(woo-yah)* . . . . crow
wǔyè *(woo-yeh)* . . . . midnight
wǔyī láodòng jié *(woo-yee)(lao-dohng)(jee-eh)* . . . . .Labor Day (May 1)
wǔyuè *(woo-yoo-eh)* . . . . May

X

xī *(ssee)* . . . . west
xǐ *(ssee)* . . . . to wash, washes, wash
xià *(ssee-ah)* . . . . .down
xiàbiān *(ssee-ah-bee-ahn)* . . . . under, below
xiàbiānde *(ssee-ah-bee-ahn-duh)* . . . . below
xiàn *(ssee-ahn)* . . . . line
114 xiàng *(ssee-ahng)* . . . . to want, wants, want

xiǎng yào *(ssee-ahng)(yow)* . . . . would like
xiānshēng *(ssee-ahn-shuhng)* . . . . Mr., sir
xiāngzi *(ssee-ahng-zuh)* . . . . trunk, suitcase
xiànzài *(ssee-ahn-zi)* . . . . .now
xiǎo *(ssee-ow)* . . . . .small
xiǎo chīdiàn *(ssee-ow)(chr-dee-ahn)* . . . . .snack shop
xiǎohái *(ssee-ow-hi)* . . . . child, children
xiǎojiě *(ssee-ow-jee-eh)* . . . . Miss
xiǎoshí *(ssee-ow-shr)* . . . . hour
xiāròu hún tūn *(ssee-ah-roh)(hoon)(toon)* . . . . .shrimp and vegetables in a wrapper, boiled
xiàtiān *(ssee-ah-tee-ahn)* . . . . summer
xiàwǔ *(ssee-ah-woo)* . . . . .afternoon
xiàxuě *(ssee-ah-ssee-yoo-eh)* . . . . to snow, snow, snows
xiàyǔ *(ssee-ah-yoo)* . . . . to rain, rain, rains
Xībānyá *(ssee-bahn-yah)* . . . . Spain
xīběi *(ssee-bay)* . . . . .west-north
xībiān *(ssee-bee-ahn)* . . . . West
xiē *(ssee-eh)* . . . . several
xié *(ssee-eh)* . . . . shoes
xiě *(ssee-eh)* . . . . to write
xiě chū *(ssee-eh)(choo)* . . . . to write out
xié diàn *(ssee-eh)(dee-ahn)* . . . . shoe store
xièxie *(ssee-eh-ssee-eh)* . . . . thank you
xīfāng *(ssee-fahng)* . . . . western
xǐhuān *(ssee-hoo-ahn)* . . . . .to like
xǐjiāojuǎn *(ssee-jee-ow-joo-ahn)* . . . . . . .to develop (the) film
xǐliǎnpén *(ssee-lee-ahn-puhn)* . . . . washbasin
xīn *(sseen)* . . . . .new
xìn *(sseen)* . . . . letter
xínglǐ *(sseeng-lee)* . . . . .luggage, baggage
xínglǐ chē *(sseeng-lee)(chuh)* . . . . .baggage cart
xīngqī *(sseeng-chee)* . . . . .week
xīngqīèr *(sseeng-chee-ur)* . . . . Tuesday
xīngqīliù *(sseeng-chee-lee-oo)* . . . . Saturday
xīngqīsān *(sseeng-chee-sahn)* . . . . Wednesday
xīngqīsì *(sseeng-chee-sih)* . . . . .Thursday
xīngqītiān *(sseeng-chee-tee-ahn)* . . . . .Sunday
xīngqīwǔ *(sseeng-chee-woo)* . . . . Friday
xīngqīyī *(sseeng-chee-yee)* . . . . Monday
Xīnxīlán *(sseen-ssee-lahn)* . . . . New Zealand
xìnyòngkǎ *(sseen-yohng-kah)* . . . . .credit card
xiōngzhào *(ssee-wong-jow)* . . . . bra
xìpiào *(ssee-pee-ow)* . . . . theater ticket
xǐyī diàn *(ssee-yee)(dee-ahn)* . . . . laundry
xǐyīfú *(ssee-yee-foo)* . . . . to do laundry
xìyuàn *(ssee-yoo-ahn)* . . . . .theater
xǐzǎo *(ssee-zow)* . . . . to bathe
xīzhuāng *(ssee-jwahng)* . . . . suit
xuěhuā *(ssee-oo-eh-hwah)* . . . . .snowflake
xuéxí *(ssee-yoo-eh-ssee)* . . . . to learn, learns, learn
xuéxiào *(ssee-yoo-eh-ssee-ow)* . . . . .school
xuēzi *(ssee-yoo-eh-zuh)* . . . . boots
xūyào *(ssee-oo-yow)* . . . . to need, needs, need

Y

yā *(yah)* . . . . duck
yágāo *(yah-gow)* . . . . toothpaste
yán *(yahn)* . . . . salt
yángròu *(yahng-roh)* . . . . .mutton
yǎnjìng *(yahn-jeeng)* . . . . eyeglasses
yánsè *(yahn-suh)* . . . . color
yào *(yow)* . . . . to want, must
yào diàn *(yow)(dee-ahn)* . . . . pharmacy
yáoyǐ *(yow-yee)* . . . . .rocking chair
yáshuā *(yah-shwah)* . . . . toothbrush

yě (*yuh*) . . . . also
yè (*yeh*) . . . . page
yèlǐ (*yeh-lee*) . . . . night
yī, yì, yí (*yee*) . . . . one
yī (*yee*) . . . . clothing
yǐ (*yee*) . . . . chair
Yí lù píng ān! (*yee*)(*loo*)(*peeng*)(*ahn*) . . . . safe and peaceful journey
yí xià (*yee*)(*ssee-ah*) . . . . a little while
yìbǎi (*yee-by*) . . . . one hundred
yīchú (*yee-choo*) . . . . clothes closet
Yìdàlì (*yee-dah-lee*) . . . . Italy
yìdiǎn (*yee-dee-ahn*) . . . . a little
yīfu (*yee-foo*) . . . . clothes
yígòng (*yee-gohng*) . . . . altogether
Yìndù (*yeen-doo*) . . . . India
Yìndùníxīyà (*yeen-doo-nee-ssee-yah*) . . . Indonesia
yīng (*yeeng*) . . . . eagle
yīnggāi (*yeeng-gi*) . . . . to have to, should
Yīngguó (*yeeng-gwoh*) . . . . England
Yīngguó rén (*yeeng-gwoh*)(*ruhn*) . . . . British
yīngwǔ (*yeeng-woo*) . . . . parrot
Yīngwén (*yeeng-wuhn*) . . . . English
yínháng (*yeen-hahng*) . . . . bank
yǐnliào (*yeen-lee-ow*) . . . . beverages
yínqì (*yeen-chee*) . . . . silver
yìqiān (*yee-chee-ahn*) . . . . one thousand
yīshēng (*yee-shuhng*) . . . . doctor
yíyàng (*yee-yahng*) . . . . same
yīyuàn (*yee-yoo-ahn*) . . . . hospital
yīyuè (*yee-yoo-eh*) . . . . January
yǐzi (*yee-zuh*) . . . . chair
yìzhí zǒu (*yee-jihr*)(*zoh*) . . . . straight ahead
yǒu (*yoh*) . . . . to have, has, have
yǒu (*yoh*) . . . . there is, there are
yòu (*yoh*) . . . . right
yòubiān (*yoh-bee-ahn*) . . . . right side
yóujú (*yoh-joo*) . . . . post office
yóupiào (*yoh-pee-ow*) . . . . stamp
yǒuqián (*yoh-chee-en*) . . . . rich
yǒurén (*yoh-ruhn*) . . . . occupied
yóutǒng (*yoh-twong*) . . . . mailbox
yǒuyìsi (*yoh-yee-see*) . . . . interesting
yóuyǒngyī (*yoh-yohng-yee*) . . . . swimsuit
yóuzhèng (*yoh-jung*) . . . . postal
yú (*yoo*) . . . . fish
yú diàn (*yoo*)(*dee-ahn*) . . . . fish store
yuán (*yoo-ahn*) . . . . unit of Chinese currency
yuánzhūbǐ (*yoo-ahn-joo-bee*) . . . . ballpoint pen
yuè (*yoo-eh*) . . . . month
yuèbào (*yoo-eh-bao*) . . . . monthly magazine
yuèliang (*yoo-eh-lee-ahng*) . . . . moon
Yuènán (*yoo-eh-nahn*) . . . . Vietnam
yuèsè (*yoo-eh-suh*) . . . . moonlight
yuètái (*yoo-eh-tie*) . . . . platform
yuèyè (*yoo-eh-yeh*) . . . . moonlit night
yùgāng (*yoo-gahng*) . . . . bath
yùndòng yòngpǐn (*yoon-dohng*)(*yohng-peen*) . . sporting goods
yùndòngxié (*yoon-dohng-ssee-eh*) . . . . . . tennis shoes
yùshì (*yoo-shr*) . . . . bathroom
yǔyī (*yoo-yee*) . . . . raincoat
yùyuē (*yoo-yoo-eh*) . . . . reservation

Z

zài (*zi*) . . . . is, are (in, at)

zài shuō yíbiàn (*zi*)(*shwoh*)(*yee-bee-ahn*) . . . .
. . . . to repeat, say once again
zài yòubiān (*zi*)(*yoh-bee-ahn*) . . . . on the right side
zài zuǒbiān (*zi*)(*zwoh-bee-ahn*) . . . . on the left side
zàijiàn (*zi-jee-ahn*) . . . . good-bye, see you again
zǎofàn (*zow-fahn*) . . . . breakfast
zázhì (*zah-jihr*) . . . . magazine
zěnme (*zuhn-muh*) . . . . how
zěnme yàng (*zuhn-muh*)(*yahng*) . . . . how
zhá (*jah*) . . . . deep-fried
zhàn (*jahn*) . . . . stop, station
zhāng (*jahng*) . . . . sheet, flat (M)
zhàng (*jahng*) . . . . account, bill
zhǎnlǎnguǎn (*jahn-lahn-gwahn*) . . . . exhibition hall
zhǎo (*jow*) . . . . to look for
zhàopiàn (*jow-pee-ahn*) . . . . photo
zhàoxiàng yòngpǐn (*jow-ssee-ahng*)(*yohng-peen*) . . . cameras
zhàoxiàngjī (*jow-ssee-ahng-jee*) . . . . camera
zhè (*juh*) . . . . this, these
zhèi (*juh-ay*) . . . . this, these
zhēng (*jung*) . . . . steamed
zhèngquède (*jung-choo-eh-duh*) . . . . correct
zhěntóu (*juhn-toh*) . . . . pillow
zhèr (*juhr*) . . . . here
zhèxiē (*juh-ssee-eh*) . . . . these
zhǐ (*jihr*) . . . . paper
zhǐ (*jihr*) . . . . only
zhǐbì (*jihr-bee*) . . . . paper currency
zhīdào (*jihr-dow*) . . . . to know, knows, know
zhōng (*jwong*) . . . . clock
zhōngbiǎo (*jwong-bee-ow*) . . . . clocks and watches
zhōngbiǎo diàn (*jwong-bee-ow*)(*dee-ahn*) . . . . . watchmakers
Zhōngguó (*jwong-gwoh*) . . . . China
Zhōngguóde (*jwong-gwoh-duh*) . . . . Chinese
Zhōngwén (*jwong-wuhn*) . . . . Chinese language
zhōngwǔ (*jwong-woo*) . . . . noon
zhōngyāng gōngyuán (*jwong-yahng*)(*gohng-yoo-ahn*) . . . . . .
. . . . central park
zhòngyào (*jwong-yow*) . . . . important
zhǔ (*joo*) . . . . boiled
zhù (*joo*) . . . . to live, reside
zhù nǐ shùnlì (*joo*)(*nee*)(*shoon-lee*) . . . . . . wish you good luck
zhuǎn (*jwahn*) . . . . to turn
zhuànyǐ (*jwahn-yee*) . . . . swivel chair
zhūbǎo (*joo-bao*) . . . . jewelry
zhuōzi (*jwoh-zuh*) . . . . table
zhūròu (*joo-roh*) . . . . pork
zì (*zih*) . . . . Chinese character
zìdiǎn (*zih-dee-ahn*) . . . . character dictionary
zìtiáo (*zih-tee-ow*) . . . . note
zìmǔ (*zih-moo*) . . . . letters of the alphabet
zìmù (*zih-moo*) . . . . subtitles
zìxíngchē (*zih-sseeng-chuh*) . . . . bicycle
zìzhǐlǒu (*zih-jihr-loh*) . . . . wastepaper basket
zōngjiào (*zwong-jee-ow*) . . . . religion
zòngzi (*zwong-zuh*) . . . . stuffed, sweet rice
zuànshí (*zwahn-shr*) . . . . diamond
zǔfù (*zoo-foo*) . . . . grandfather
zǔfùmǔ (*zoo-foo-moo*) . . . . grandparents
zǔmǔ (*zoo-moo*) . . . . grandmother
zuǒ (*zwoh*) . . . . left
zuò (*zwoh*) . . . . by, via
zuò (*zwoh*) . . . . to sit, ride in
zuǒbiān (*zwoh-bee-ahn*) . . . . left side
zuótiān (*zwoh-tee-ahn*) . . . . yesterday
zuòwèi (*zwoh-way*) . . . . seat **115**

This beverage guide is intended to explain the variety of beverages available to you while **zài Zhōngguó.** It is by no means complete. Some of the experimenting has been left up to you, but this should get you started.

Chá (tea)

hóng chá . . . . black tea
   lìzhī hóng chá . . . . . . litchi black tea

hóng chá jiā niúnǎi . . . tea with milk
níngméng chá . . . . tea with lemon
lǜ chá . . . . green tea
wūlóng chá . . . . fermented tea
mòlìhuà chá . . . . jasmine tea
qīng chá . . . . plain tea

Jiǔ (wine)

pútáojiǔ . . . . grape wine
hóng pútáojiǔ . . . . red wine
bái pútáojiǔ . . . . white wine
huángjiǔ . . . . rice wine from
               Shàoxīng area
xiāngbīn . . . . champagne

Píjiǔ (beer)

hēi píjiǔ . . . . black beer

(gahn-bay)
Gānbēi!
cheers

Lièjiǔ (spirits)

báilándì . . . . brandy
wēishìjì . . . . whisky
lǎngmǔjiǔ . . . . rum
fútèjiā . . . . vodka
dùsōngzǐjiǔ . . . . gin
gāoliángjiǔ . . . . sorghum spirits
zhúyèqīng . . . . very strong Chinese
              spirits
lǜdào shāojiǔ . . . . very strong spirits
máotáijiǔ . . . . spirits from
              Guìzhōu area
fénjiǔ . . . . spirits from
              Shānxī area

Qítā Yǐnliào (other beverages)

lěng yǐn . . . . cold drink
qìshuǐ . . . . soft drink, lemonade
kuàngquán shuǐ . . . . . . mineral water
sūdǎshuǐ . . . . soda water
kāishuǐ . . . . boiled water
shuǐguǒ zhī . . . . fruit juice
júzishuǐ . . . . orange juice
píngguǒ zhī . . . . apple juice
kěkǒukělè . . . . Coca Cola
bǎishì kělè . . . . Pepsi Cola
kāfēi . . . . coffee
kāfēi jiā niúnǎi . . . . coffee with cream
niúnǎi . . . . milk
lěng niúnǎi . . . . cold milk
kěkě . . . . cocoa
rè qiǎokèlì . . . . hot chocolate
suān méi tāng . . . . soft drink (made
              from dried prunes,
              sugar and spices)

Bīngkuài . . . . ice cubes

Càidān
menu guide

菜单

Zuò Fǎ (ways of preparation)

做法

miàntuō	in batter
zhǔ	boiled
kǎo	baked
shāo	roasted
zhēng	steamed
zhá	fried, deep-fried
chǎo	stir-fried, sautéed
kǎo	broiled

Shuǐguǒ (fruit)

水果

júzi	orange
lízi	plum, pear
táozi	peach
xiāngjiāo	banana
mìjú	tangerine
mángguǒ	mango
wúhuāguǒ	fig
lìzhī	litchi
yīngtáo	cherries
píngguǒ	apple
méizi	prune
pútáo	grapes
zǎozi	dates
níngméng	lemon
cǎoméi	strawberries
mùméi	raspberries
xìngzi	apricot
yēzi	coconut
shìzi	persimmon
bōluó	pineapple

FOLD HERE

点心

Diǎnxīn (snacks)

dòu shā bāo	steamed bun with red-bean paste
cài bāo	steamed bun with vegetables
zhī má bǐng	sesame crisp cake
básī píngguǒ	hot-candied apple

饭面

Miàn Fàn (rice and noodles)

bái fàn	plain rice
dàn chǎo fàn	fried rice with egg
jīsī miàn	noodles with shredded chicken
ròusī miàn	noodles with shredded pork
xiārén miàn	noodles with shrimp
dōnggū miàn	noodles with mushrooms
zhūgān miàn	noodles with pork liver
sùcài miàn	noodles with vegetables
chǎo miàn	fried noodles
xiārén chǎo miàn	fried noodles with shrimp

(chr-fahn)
Chīfàn
let's eat

蔬菜

Shūcài (vegetables)

dòuyá	bean sprouts
càihuā	cauliflower
sǔn	bamboo sprouts
cōng	green onions
jiāng	ginger
qíncài	celery
báicài	cabbage
bōcài	spinach
mógū	mushrooms
huángguā	cucumbers
biǎndòu	beans
wāndòu	peas
shēngcài	lettuce

凉盘

Lěng Pán (appetizers)

bái qiē jī	cold chicken
wǔxiāng yā	spicy duck
yóu bào xiā	oil-fried shrimps
xūn yú	smoked fish
wǔxiāng niúròu	spiced beef
xián dàn	pickled salted egg
yánshuǐ yā	salted duck
bàn hǎizhé	fish jelly
là cài	hot, pickled mustard greens
xián huā shēng	salted peanuts

汤

Tāng (soup)

dàn huā tāng	egg-flower soup
báicài tāng	cabbage soup
xīhóngshì dàn tāng	tomato and egg soup
dōngguā tāng	white gourd soup
niúròu tāng	beef soup
xièròu tāng	crab soup
jī tāng	chicken soup
bèiké tāng	scallop soup
zhàcài tāng	pickled vegetable soup

Tiáowèiliào (seasoning)

yán	salt
hújiāo	pepper
yóu	oil
cù	vinegar
jièmo	mustard
jiàng yóu	soy sauce
táng	sugar
xiāng yóu	sesame oil
suàn	garlic
làjiāo yóu	pepper oil
làjiāo fěn	chili pepper

Zhūròu (pork)

tángcù páigǔ	sweet-and-sour spareribs
tángcù lǐjī	sweet-and-sour pork
shīzi tóu	pork meatballs
qīngjiāo ròusī	pork with green pepper
yúxiāng ròusī	spicy shredded pork
gānzhá zhūpái	fried pork fillet
chǎo zhūgān	stir-fried pork liver
chǎo yāohuār	stir-fried kidney

Niúròu (beef)

tángcù niúròu wán	sweet-and-sour meatballs
chǎo niúròu	stir-fried beef
gānbiān niúròu sī	dry-stir-fried beef
niúròu yángcōng	fried beef with onions
lóngxū niúròu	beef stew in soy sauce
hóngshāo niúròu	sliced beef with asparagus
gālí niúròu	curried beef
Měnggǔ kǎo ròu	Mongolian barbecue
háoyóu niúròu	beef with oyster sauce
qīngjiāo niúròu	shredded beef with peppers

Jīyā (poultry)

jī	chicken
yā	duck
chún	quail
yějī	pheasant
huǒjī	turkey
é	goose
gēzi	pigeon
chǎo jī sī	fried chicken shreds
gālí jī	curried chicken
yāoguǒ jīdīng	diced chicken with cashews
jī sī chǎo sǔn	fried chicken with bamboo shoots
zhāngchá yā	fried duck in spices
kǎo yā	roasted duck
cuìpí yā	crispy duck

Yǐnliào (beverages)

chá	tea
kāfēi	coffee
niúnǎi	milk
jiǔ	wine
píjiǔ	beer
shuǐ	water
kuàngquán shuǐ	mineral water
júzishuǐ	orange juice

Hǎixiān (seafood)

tǎyú	sole
guìyú	salmon
jìyú	perch
xuěyú	cod
lǐyú	carp
píngyú	turbot
pángxiè	crab
háo	oysters
xiān gānbèi	scallops
xiā	shrimp
lóngxiā	lobster
dàxiā	prawns
zhá dàxiā	fried shrimp
pēng dàxiā	braised prawns
zhá yú tiáo	fried fish slices
tángcù yú	sweet-and-sour fish
hóngshāo yú	sautéed fish in soy sauce
qīngzhēng yú	steamed Mandarin fish
tángcù huángyú	sweet-and-sour yellow fish
qīngzhēng xiè	steamed crab
xièfěn càixīn	crab with vegetables
miàntuō xiè	fried crab in batter
fúróng xiè	crab with egg
gōngbào xiārén	shrimp with hot peppers
xiè ròu dòufu	crabmeat with soy sauce

Dòu Fǔ (bean curd)

hóngshāo dòufu	bean curd with soy sauce
mápó dòufu	bean curd with pepper
dònggū dòufu	bean curd with mushrooms
xiārén dòufu	bean curd with shrimp
mápó dòufu	bean curd with minced pork in hot sauce
shāguō dòufu	bean curd in casserole

FOLD HERE

FOLD HERE

(woh)
wǒ

(woh-muhn)
wǒmen

(nee)
nǐ

(nee-muhn)
nǐmen

(tah)
tā

(tah-muhn)
tāmen

(lie)
lái

(woh) *(lie)*
wǒ lái

(ssee-yoo-eh-ssee)
xuéxí

(woh) *(ssee-yoo-eh-ssee)*
wǒ xuéxí

(choo)
qù

(woh) *(choo)*
wǒ qù

(yoh)
yǒu

(woh) *(yoh)*
wǒ yǒu

(ssee-ahng) *(yow)*
xiǎng yào

(woh) *(ssee-ahng)* *(yow)*
wǒ xiǎng yào

(ssee-oo-yow)
xūyào

(woh) *(ssee-oo-yow)*
wǒ xūyào

we	I
you (plural)	you (singular)
they	he, she, it
to learn	to come
I learn	I come
to have	to go (to)
I have	I go (to)
to need	would like
I need	I would like

(jee-ow)
jiào

(woh)   *(jee-ow)*
wǒ jiào

(my)
mǎi

(woh)   *(my)*
wǒ mǎi

(shwoh)
shuō

(woh)   *(shwoh)*
wǒ shuō

(joo)
zhù

(woh)   *(joo)*
wǒ zhù

(jee-ow)
jiào

(woh)   *(jee-ow)*
wǒ jiào

(teeng-lee-oo)
tíngliú

(woh)   *(teeng-lee-oo)*
wǒ tíngliú

(chr)
chī

(woh)   *(chr)*
wǒ chī

(huh)
hē

(woh)   *(huh)*
wǒ hē

(shwoh)
shuō

(woh)   *(shwoh)*
wǒ shuō

(my)
mài

(woh)   *(my)*
wǒ mài

(dwong)
dǒng

(woh)   *(dwong)*
wǒ dǒng

(zi)   *(shwoh)*   *(yee-bee-ahn)*
zài shuō yíbiàn

(woh)   *(zi)*   *(shwoh)*   *(yee-bee-ahn)*
wǒ zài shuō yíbiàn

to buy	to be called / named
I buy	my name is
to live / reside	to speak
I live / reside	I speak
to stay	to order
I stay	I order
to drink	to eat
I drink	I eat
to sell	to say
I sell	I say
to repeat	to understand
I repeat	I understand

(jow)
zhǎo

(woh) *(jow)*
wǒ zhǎo

(kahn-jee-ahn)
kànjiàn

(woh) *(kahn-jee-ahn)*
wǒ kànjiàn

(jee)
jì

(woh) *(jee)*
wǒ jì

(shway)
shuì

(woh) *(shway)*
wǒ shuì

(dah) *(dee-ahn-hwah)*
dǎ diànhuà

(woh) *(dah)* *(dee-ahn-hwah)*
wǒ dǎ diànhuà

(foo) *(chee-ahn)*
fù qián

(woh) *(foo)* *(chee-ahn)*
wǒ fù qián

(gay)
gěi

(woh) *(gay)*
wǒ gěi

(ssee-eh)
xiě

(woh) *(ssee-eh)*
wǒ xiě

(kahn)
kàn

(woh) *(kahn)*
wǒ kàn

(nung)
néng

(woh) *(nung)*
wǒ néng

(yeeng-gi)
yīnggāi

(woh) *(yeeng-gi)*
wǒ yīnggāi

(jihr-dow)
zhīdào

(woh) *(jihr-dow)*
wǒ zhīdào

to see	to look for
I see	I look for
to sleep	to send by mail
I sleep	I send by mail
to pay	to make a telephone call
I pay	I make a telephone call
to write	to give
I write	I give
to be able to / can	to read / look at
I can	I read / look at
to know	to have to / should
I know	I have to / should

(ki)
kāi

(woh) *(ki)*
wǒ kāi

(fay)
fēi

(woh) *(fay)*
wǒ fēi

(loo-sseeng)
lǚxíng

(woh) *(loo-sseeng)*
wǒ lǚxíng

(zwoh)
zuò

(woh) *(zwoh)*
wǒ zuò

(hwahn) *(chuh)*
huàn chē

(woh) *(hwahn)* *(chuh)*
wǒ huàn chē

(dow)
dào

(woh) *(dow)*
wǒ dào

(shoh-shr)
shōushi

(woh) *(shoh-shr)*
wǒ shōushi

(ssee)
xǐ

(woh) *(ssee)*
wǒ xǐ

(deeng)
dìng

(woh) *(deeng)*
wǒ dìng

(shr)
shì

(woh) *(shr)*
wǒ shì

(gay) *(woh)*
gěi wǒ . . .

(dee-oo)
diū

(woh) *(dee-oo)*
wǒ diū

125

to fly

I fly

to sit / ride in

I sit / ride in

to arrive

I arrive

to wash

I wash

to be

I am

to lose

I lose

to leave / depart

I leave / depart

to travel

I travel

to transfer (vehicles)

I transfer (vehicles)

to pack

I pack

to book / reserve

I book / reserve

give me . . .

(jeen-tee-ahn)
jīntiān

(nee)   *(how)*   *(mah)*
Nǐ hǎo ma?

(zwoh-tee-ahn)
zuótiān

(cheeng)
qǐng

(meeng-tee-ahn)
míngtiān

(ssee-eh-ssee-eh)
xièxie

(zi-jee-ahn)
zàijiàn

(dway-boo-chee)
duìbùqǐ

(lao)   *(sseen)*
lǎo – xīn

(dwoh-shao)   *(chee-ahn)*
Duōshao qián?

(dah)   *(ssee-ow)*
dà – xiǎo

(ki)   *(gwahn)*
kāi – guān

How are you?	today
please	yesterday
thank you	tomorrow
excuse me / I'm sorry	good-bye
How much does this cost?	old - new
open - closed	big - small

(jee-ahn-kahng) *(beeng)*
jiànkāng – bìng

(how) *(hwhy)* *(boo)* *(how)*
hǎo – huài / bù hǎo

(ruh) *(lung)*
rè – lěng

(dwahn) *(chahng)*
duǎn – cháng

(gao) *(dee)*
gāo – dī

(shahng) *(ssee-ah)*
shàng – xià

(zwoh) *(yoh)*
zuǒ – yòu

(mahn) *(kwhy)*
màn – kuài

(lao) *(nee-ahn-cheeng)*
lǎo – niánqīng

(gway) *(pee-ahn-yee)*
guì – piányí

(chee-oong) *(yoh-chee-en)*
qióng – yǒuqián

(dwoh) *(shao)*
duō – shǎo

good - bad	healthy - sick
short - long	hot - cold
up - down	high - low
slow - fast	left - right
expensive- inexpensive	old - young
a lot - a little	poor - rich

Now that you've finished...

You've done it!

You've completed all the Steps, stuck your labels, flashed your cards, cut out your beverage and menu guides and practiced your new language. Do you realize how far you've come and how much you've learned? You've accomplished what it could take years to achieve in a traditional language class.

You can now confidently

- ask questions,
- understand directions,
- make reservations,
- order food and
- shop for anything.

And you can do it all in a foreign language! Go anywhere with confidence — from a large cosmopolitan restaurant to a small, out-of-the-way village where no one speaks English. Your experiences will be much more enjoyable and worry-free now that you speak the language.

As you've seen, learning a foreign language can be fun. Why limit yourself to just one? Now you're ready to learn another language with the *10 minutes a day®* Series!

Kris Kershul

Kristine Kershul

To place an order –

- Visit us at **www.bbks.com**, day or night.
- Call us at (800) 488-5068 or (206) 284-4211 between 8:00 a.m. and 5:00 p.m. Pacific Time, Monday - Friday.
- If you have questions about ordering, please call us. You may also fax us at (206) 284-3660 or email us at customer.service@bbks.com.